OUR FATHER

A Tribute to Dermot Morgan

OUR FATHER

A Tribute to Dermot Morgan

Don, Bobby and Ben Morgan

New Island Books
Dublin

Our Father: A Tribute to Dermot Morgan
First published November 1998 by
New Island Books
2 Brookside
Dundrum Road
Dublin 14
Ireland

British Library Cataloguing in Publication Data
A catalogue record for this book is available from the British
Library

ISBN 1 874597 96 0

**New Island Books receives financial assistance from The Arts
Council (An Chomhairle Ealaíon), Dublin, Ireland.**

Grateful acknowledgement is made to all those who gave
permission to use photographs contained within the book and to
the *Sunday Tribune* for permission to reproduce articles by Dermot
Morgan which appeared in that newspaper during the 1980s. The
publishers have made every reasonable effort to contact the
copyright holders of material produced in this book. If any
involuntary infringement of copyright has occurred, sincere
apologies are offered and the owners of such copyright are
requested to contact the publishers.

Cover design: Slick Fish Design, Dublin
Typesetting: New Island Books
Printed in Ireland by Colour Books, Ltd.

Contents

Acknowledgements

The compilation of this book was almost always an absolute joy for us. This was because of the many different and wonderful people who kindly gave us some of their time to help in making this a work we can look back on with pride.

We'd like to thank them all and acknowledge their help. Firstly there are those among our family and particularly close friends of our father's — Susanne Morgan (for reminding us of deadlines), Fiona Clarke (for shovelling scripts and pictures our way), Ben (for being as bonkers as he is — we love you), Denise Morgan (for her lovely piece), Paul Morgan (for explanations and psychiatric consultations), Donagh Morgan (for writing such a wonderful Afterword), Pat Finn (for the excellent Foreword), Eoin Morgan (for being there), Michael Redmond (for taking our calls), and Peter Redmond (for reminiscing from time to time) and Robbie O'Connell (for making time when over from America).

Also deserving of our thanks for helping to bring this book into being are Barry Devlin, Michael Paul Gallagher, Gerry Stembridge (the first person we interviewed), Paddy Hehir, Ak Kennedy, John Fisher, Professor Terence Dolan, John Keogh, Shay Healy, Larry Masterson, Fiona Looney, Declan Lowney, Pat Kenny, Hillary at *Kenny Live*, Barry Meggs (the Bitch in the Kitchen), Leo Speßhardt, Michael Donald, Liam Mackay, Niall Stokes, Paddy Murray, Sam Smyth, Ardal O'Hanlon, Pauline McLynn, Ciara Considine, Niamh Sweeney, Joe Joyce and Edwin Higel.

Our apologies to those we did not get an opportunity to speak to: we tried our best to make sure that your roles in Dermot's life were documented.

This book follows, in broadly chronological form, Dermot's life and career, interspersed with samples of his work at different times. Rather than try and write it together — an impossible task — we split it up and the main chronological chapters, (those without an author's name on them) as well as the introductions to the scripts were written by Don.

To Pops —

the best is yet to come . . .

FOREWORD

by Pat Finn

To lose a comic genius is a huge loss for Ireland and for many who enjoyed his humour, and a much greater loss to his family. But to lose your drinking partner is surely the greatest loss. Dermot and I had taken in all the great venues: Dublin, London, Carrick, Amsterdam, Copenhagen, Dingle, Pisa and Galway, and a few more between. Dying so young was uncharacteristic — his timing was never so far out and he definitely never left a party so early. We had solved all the world's problems, and our own, with a pint over the last quarter-century. To take you back...

It was one of those misty early autumnal nights, I think perhaps September to October 1976, and Dermot and I were in front of the committee of Blackrock College RFC in Dublin with our presentation to take over the running of the Saturday night dance. We were prepared — Dermot had a pipe for *gravitas* and I had borrowed my father's Austin 1100; we also wore ties — a picture of businessmen on the move. We outlined that we had virtually run the very successful University College Dublin Saturday night disco on the Belfield campus between us (i.e. Dermot had a loose attachment to the committee which ran it and I had regularly paid in). Dermot performed a masterful display of salesmanship, extolling our reliability and experience and the fact that we knew every potential punter and every

Guard in Blackrock, while all the while reassembling, blowing, sucking and re-lighting his pipe. To this day, I remember it as a great performance, even if we were politely shown the door. We didn't get the gig, Blackrock lost out on huge revenues and were subsequently reduced to hiring journeymen New Zealand players. They had their chance.

I tell the story because, while I would not persist in the entertainment world, Dermot had to — it was a way of life for him as well as a career. Any setback was immediately replaced by the next plan, accompanied by printing, posters, and a belief. I remember one of his earliest gigs on a Sunday morning in a working mans' club in Dublin, where no one listened to a word, or if they did it was through raised *News of the World* papers. Silence to all material — enough to disillusion most, but not Dermot. Ever onwards.

I had met Dermot two years before, and we immediately became close friends. From the time I met him, I understood where he wanted to get to in his life. I would love to say I never doubted he would get there — I did many times. Not because of a lack of ability or talent, but because of the distance to be covered: local boy in Mount Merrion, South Dublin with a strong aversion to travel (which permitted him only to go to the pub at the end of his road for a drink, and no further) to become international comic success, this was his aim. Many will remember the shows in UCD — I still have some Big Gom posters at home — and I think of the jump between those and the hundred-foot posters outside Waterloo Station and how it started with photocopies being put up with drawing pins. He always knew he'd make it — 'Taxis in London, Pat' was his marker; when we'd reached that, we would have made it (I would agree — 'we'll be driving them!'). Well, Dermot got his taxis, and chauffeurs, in London and to that extent fulfilled his ambition. The thing is, such was his momentum at the time he died, he could have owned several taxi firms within two years. And this is the real tragedy of his professional life, not what he did achieve but what he was about to go on to do. We are all poorer for that. They say you don't miss what you don't know — well, I do. I want to know his next plan, next character, next plot and his resolute belief in them.

The purpose of this book is to provide an insight into the life of Dermot Morgan, through the recollections of his sons, Don, Bobby and Ben, and of his many friends. Whatever the final outcome, I have to say that to know him you had to meet him, to feel the life force coming from him; his love of life and people, of entertaining... and being entertained. He was both a very public man and a very private man — and sometimes the public didn't realise this and he promptly put them straight. Sometimes we, the private section, got it wrong and were put straight as well. Dermot's too short life, like the great sport of hurling, does not easily translate to print, so it is a credit to his sons Don, Bobby and Ben, and his friends who contributed to this book, that such a wonderful insight and profile is provided here.

IN THE BEGINNING

Our father, Dermot John Morgan, first saw the light of day in Dublin on the 31st of March, 1952. His parents, Donnchadh and Holly Morgan, already had two daughters, Denise and Ruth, by the time he was born and Dermot was their first son. Their younger son, Paul, was born a few years later in 1958. They lived in a bungalow which is still occupied by some of us Morgans in Mount Merrion, at the time a growing suburb of Dublin, quite near Blackrock and Stillorgan to the south of the city. It nestles close to the foothills of the Dublin mountains and has some spectacular views over Dublin Bay.

Donnchadh and Holly were interesting characters in their own right and their lives and personalities give some hint of the flavour of Dermot's early life and where his personality and gifts came from, in part.

I never met my grandfather, Donnchadh. He died in 1974, some time before any of us were born. He was a big-ish guy from Thurles in County Tipperary whose father, Denis, had been active in the War of Independence in the early 1920s. Donnchadh worked in Dublin as a civil servant, and was apparently gifted in different fields and disciplines. He was artistic... well, sort of. He wasn't Salvador Dali, but he was nevertheless an enthusiastic amateur with quite a bit of talent. By the end, he wasn't just making use of his talent for simple sketching but was also sculpting. Donnchadh enjoyed a wide variety of other pastimes as well and took a liking to sporty things, such as swimming, cycling and, I think, even cross-country running.

From the pictures we have and those relatives have shown me over the years, it's pretty safe to say his appearance wasn't entirely unlike Dermot's. In fact, in some pictures, the similarity is striking. He had a shock of premature white hair, far whiter than Dermot's would eventually be, and his face and build hinted towards an ageing film star. However, he apparently used to play down his appearance by describing himself, according to our aunt, Denise, as 'attractively ugly'.

He had a particular sense of theatre and an outlook on life which sometimes led to strangely comic moments. There was one particular story Dermot loved to tell us about the time his dad left the house for work one morning as the milkman was making his rounds. Donnchadh was upset over something or with someone and was therefore more than a little engrossed in his own thoughts. He didn't drive at that stage and usually cycled to his office in the centre of Dublin at, I think, the Office of Public Works on St Stephen's Green. He was just outside the gate of the house, busy trying to affix his bicycle clips to his ankles, when the milkman's pony, which was standing out on the road as his master delivered the milk, took notice of this sight and went over to him to see what he was doing. The pony peered over Donnchadh's shoulder to get a closer look, which frightened the life out of him. As he turned in a reflex reaction, he managed to deck the poor animal! Unsurprisingly, the milkman was not impressed.

Although our grandfather died before any of us were born, Bobby and myself had the pleasure of growing up with our grandmother, Holly, for the first twelve or so years of our lives, until she died in November 1991. She originally came from Dun Laoghaire, which was then known as

Kingstown, in County Dublin. She told us a bit about her childhood over the years. She came from a mixed religious background: her father, whose surname was Stokes, was a Catholic and her mother was a Protestant. Holly had a bit of a rebellious streak in her when she was growing up. Her father apparently didn't like football, calling it 'that gurriers' game', and forbidding Holly from going to any matches. But she went anyway and, she told me once, was friendly with a German who played for the famous Dublin club, Bohemians, at that time. The story, as she told it, ended tragically: the German was injured by the stud of a football boot, the wound became infected, and he died.

The most striking thing about Holly was that she was an astonishingly brilliant mimic. She'd take off anyone, with a venomous sense of humour. Neighbours, friends, even family on occasion, would all be in the firing line. She'd identify a particularly striking element of a person's character — a biting tone to a voice or a particular demeanour — and exaggerate it. I remember sitting in her kitchen in the house up the road from us where she lived at the time, listening to her imitate people I knew well, and watching her make something very funny out of their characteristics.

She certainly wasn't a conventional Granny, in fact she hated that title: she wanted to be called Holly or Hilda or Gran — anything but Granny. She had a kind of adolescent humour — extraordinarily black but nevertheless extremely funny — which appealed to the cheeky pre-adolescent I was at the time. She also taught us a few of the more common swear words, though I doubt that our parents were very happy about it. I'm sure Dermot got elements of his own humour from both his parents, as his dad also had a sense of humour not unlike his own. For instance, I remember him telling me about his dad's 'lavatorial' sense of humour —

fart gags and the like — which Dermot shared with him. He used to love the scene in the Mel Brooks film *Blazing Saddles* where a bunch of Hedy Lamarr's henchmen are sitting around a campfire eating beans and one by one they all fart. Dermot once said to me that he wished his dad had seen that scene (he died the year it came out in Ireland).

On another level, Dermot's schooling played a role in building up his character and his views on the world. After an initial stint in pre-school in Scoil San Treasa in Mount Merrion, he went to St Lawrence's National School for boys in Kilmacud, just a walk away from where he lived. His early childhood exposed him to things which would determine his eventual world view and the kind of person he would be, especially later on when he went to the local Christian Brothers secondary school, Oatlands College, in Stillorgan.

Dermot's upbringing and schooling was completely different to mine or Bobby's. I went to a non-denominational school and therefore I have little, if any, idea of what it is like to be educated by a church-affiliated organisation, particularly in a 1950s and 60s Ireland. However, it doesn't seem to have been particularly conducive to his having had a happy time at that stage in his life. The more severe members of staff seemed to have done their best to fill their pupils with a combination of fear and insecurity in order to keep control, encouraging a 'macho' atmosphere in the school which spread among the students as well; the kind of atmosphere in which Dermot was never at home.

In the type of school the Christian Brothers ran in those days, Dermot was always going to be a problem for some of the teachers. He clowned around a bit in class and some of the Christian Brothers took to exerting their authority over him in a way which made no allowances for the creative and less academic talents which he obviously had alongside his academic ability. He was often subjected to corporal punishment.

However, they failed to change who he was. If anything, his experiences there probably made him more determined to be himself. After he died, a former classmate told a story on radio about how one day one of the Brothers said to him: 'Morgan, you'll never make anything of yourself', to which Dermot replied, under his breath, 'You just fuckin' watch me.' I think the end result was a severe beating.

His experiences in school convinced him, and others of his generation, of some of the things that were wrong with the world and needed to be changed. Dermot's attitudes towards the Catholic Church were formed at that time. They tried to teach him religion by hammering home the concepts of eternal damnation and guilt. He didn't enjoy school: quite the opposite.

But he was a teenager in the 1960s and, like every other person growing up at that time, had other things than school in his life, notably playing football (not very well) and listening to music. Unlike most of his generation, he wasn't that interested in the Rolling Stones or the Beatles — instead he was a Beach Boys fan, idolising Brian Wilson. He got a present of a record player one Christmas but could only afford one record — the Beach Boys' album *Pet Sounds* which he brought home and began to play with great ceremony. He continued to play it over and over again until he had driven everyone else in the house almost crazy, but he never lost his love of the group. According to his cousin Donagh Morgan, Dermot had a Brian Wilson 'pose' which wasn't that far off the mark. Why he liked the Beach Boys so much and found an affinity with them was never quite clear to me. He used to explain it ironically by saying that he could relate to what the Beach Boys were singing about because he lived in cold and wet Ireland!

Donagh, who like Dermot's father also came from Thurles in County Tipperary, and Dermot spent several of their summer holidays together in Dublin in those days, as did Donagh's brother, Eoin. As Donagh remembers it:

> I'd be sent out to Blackrock but there was nothing to do in Blackrock — Aunt Peig would go to work and I'd be on my own all day. We quickly worked out that it would be more fun for me to go up to Mount Merrion and be introduced to the pleasures of smoking Consulate in the woods [near Dermot's house] and spotting young ones... 'The Barn' was the place where we went dancing, beside the church. It was a sort of a little hall. There were 'dishcos' and live bands with exotic names like 'Herbaceous Border'.

Dermot left the Christian Brothers and Oatlands in 1970 after his Leaving Certificate was completed. There was doubtless a feeling of release from what in general terms had been an unhappy time in school. This I have deduced to a large extent because, like many people, he never really discussed school with us, bar a few stories or glimpses into the happier sides of his childhood.

But he did begin to tell us in detail about his time in college, especially in the last year of his life as I entered the same college, University College Dublin, and Bobby approached his Leaving Cert and the end of his schooldays. College was where Dermot would first find people to encourage his talents and where he would discover a thirst for performing before an audience.

Before we move on to that, however, some more detail and memories of Dermot's life before he was a grown-up and a dad should be filled in. For a picture of him as a child, an adolescent and a brother, here are his sister, Denise's, recollections...

DERMOT THE BROTHER

by Denise Morgan

When I was asked if I would like to contribute to this book in the form of some anecdotes about Dermot, I gave much thought as to how any contribution I could make would convey any sense of Dermot the real person. Dermot the funny man is legendary. Everyone has an anecdote about him. OK, I could tell you plenty of them, but would you have any more idea about the real Dermot when I had finished? We all know how funny, talented and clever he was, but how many people knew the real person? So as Dermot's sister, I would like to offer a few thoughts on Dermot the brother, and perhaps a few comments about Dermot the son. Both our parents are dead and surely it's an important aspect of the man as to what kind of son he was.

I won't dwell on Dermot's childhood other than to say that despite being 'on-stage' from the word 'go', he was a sensitive and affectionate child. He was deeply affected by the death of our older sister Ruth when he was nearly five (about Ben's age as I write now). He often pondered on the events in later years.

Our house was one of huge highs and lows and was frequently hilarious. Mealtimes were a veritable ground of verbal fencing. The cut and parry was of the sharpest wit. It sometimes got too much for our father who often reminded us that mealtimes were supposed to be social occasions, not 'bear gardens'.

When we were young children, Dermot and I beat the crap out of each other. It was only when we got into our teens that the real friendship grew between us. Teen time is usually a difficult period for most of us. We feel the need for an 'us and them' divide between parents/adults and the real people — teenagers. Dermot was my ally in this great divide.

In a time when growing up and sex were huge secrets, he suggested that we pool our information about these mysteries to try and make some sense of them between us. We did this, but sadly it did not make too much sense at this time because the combined information was just too sparse.

Dermot took the academic route in life. He went to university and I joined a dance troupe in Spain. I still have some of the letters Dermot wrote to me in those days. He certainly felt that I should have solved the mysteries mentioned in the previous paragraph. He begged me to tell him all about my 'sexploits'. It has to be admitted that my 'sexploits' never got further than talking about 'it' in the dressing-rooms. But I certainly got the information — YES!

Our friendship grew throughout his university career and our young adulthood. Life at home had been for a long time somewhat like living beside an active volcano. The eruptions were fierce. When our parents finally split up (just before we were all incarcerated in lava), Dermot was the only one who could walk the political tightrope, and maintain a relationship with both parents. It has to be said that our younger brother Paul was too young to have a say in the matter — so no implied criticism Paul!

When our father died suddenly, in his early fifties, we leaned on each other. Dermot would in times of crisis put his thoughts on paper. He advised me to do the same. 'Write it down Denny, it will keep you sane.' A piece that he wrote about our father's death would draw tears from a stone.

Dermot's career had a great deal of ups-and-downs. Just making ends meet was often a struggle. This challenge never prevented him from living his life with great style and generosity. So many times he did charity gigs and refused to take any money, when he had no notion how he would pay his next utilities bill. As to style, he always said that the bank manager couldn't take back the suntan or the memories. I once asked Dermot what he would do if he won the lottery. He said he would not change his lifestyle, but he would just be solvent.

The first Christmas after our mother died, I was sad, lonely and living in London. We had just lost the business in which we had put all our hopes, not to mention our money. So I was also broke. Dermot and I, as always, kept in touch by frequent phone calls. I said how sad I was that we could not be together for Christmas. A few days later, six airline tickets arrived in the post. Then another phone call; could we manage two hundred pounds for the accommodation he had booked for us close to his house? Yes, we could. When we went to pay our bill it was for four hundred pounds, but Dermot had paid two hundred pounds of it. I was not supposed to have found this out. We had a lovely Christmas and Fiona [Dermot's partner] cooked a great Christmas dinner for everyone. I never told Dermot that I knew he had paid half the bill. He never told me he had done all this on his own overdraft. I only found that out years later.

When our mother Holly was diagnosed with terminal cancer, she only had weeks to live. Dermot was working on his radio programme *Scrap Saturday*. He used to come in to the hospital with his notebook and write scripts while he sat with her. One day I overheard a visitor say to another patient, 'You know that Dermot Morgan fellow? I never liked him myself, but if you saw the way he looks after his mother — there's good in the worst of us!' Dermot was highly amused when I told him.

Holly went into a coma on the Friday that Dermot was recording the last episode in a series of *Scrap Saturday*. I kept him updated on her condition all day by phone. When he finished the recording he joined Paul and me in our sad vigil. By 3.00 a.m. the nurse said that this could go on for days and we all looked exhausted. She suggested we go home and get some sleep. My youngest child was just a baby — I was still nursing him — so this sounded like a good idea. We all decided to go home. When we got to the front door of the hospital, Dermot turned to me and said that he had a feeling he should stay with her. So he went back in. Less than an hour later he phoned me to go back to the hospital immediately. We were all with Holly when she died. If Dermot had not stayed with her she might have died alone. I was always so grateful to him for this. At Holly's funeral Dermot read from the New Testament, Mark 14. 32:42. Will you not wait one hour with me? He was not a religious man in the accepted sense but he certainly was spiritual.

BIG GOM

College is radically different to school. It offers other, extra-curricular things to do and, generally, there's a less formal feel to it. These are all things I noticed when I first arrived in UCD in September 1997. From the conversations I had at the time with Dermot about college, I wouldn't be wholly surprised if he had similar feelings when he arrived there — on what was then UCD's new Belfield campus — for the first time in the autumn of 1970.

From the stories he told of that time, and that I heard later on when researching this book, I get the impression that college was good *craic* in those days. He found people and things to do there which offered some fun and a bit of a laugh outside of lectures. He also found new friends, people who equally wanted to create a bit of madness and mischief along with having fun.

Dermot probably hoped to some extent that his experiences in university would give him a clue as to what he would do with the rest of his life. At heart, he wanted to be a writer and a performer, but that wasn't necessarily the sort of thing that you told your friends. From some of the things he said to me when I went to college, I don't think he had the slightest notion of precisely what he was going to do while he was there. Eventually, he settled on a BA in English and Philosophy. Many of his friends didn't know exactly what they wanted to do with their lives either, and that uncertainty was probably another thing that bound them together.

There was a crowd he hung around with, who shared his attitudes. They spent hours upon hours chatting, messing around together and whiling away the time. Among his friends in college were his cousin Donagh, who also made it to UCD, Robbie O'Connell, Paddy Hehir, Declan Cashan (who was known as 'the goat'), Pat Courtney and, later on, Pat Finn. They were all into having a laugh and a good time: it wasn't school anymore, and they were going to take advantage of university's freedoms and opportunities. As a result, he and his mates tended to enjoy passing the hours of free time they allowed themselves; by goofing around and contemplating finer, intellectual issues. Donagh describes some of what they did:

> We used to hang out, solve all the problems of the world, fantasise about young ones. We played music: it was great to have Robbie (O'Connell) and Paddy (Hehir) around: two guitarists in our midst, and both writing their own stuff as well. Most of the hanging out was done in the canteen where we used to drink that awful Belfield coffee. Hours were spent sitting and chatting: we'd go for lunch and spend our time there, for three or four hours in the afternoon. A lot of talking and discovering of the meaning of life was done in that situation.

During his college years Dermot was known to his friends by the nickname 'German'. Why, or where it came from, is now difficult to pin down. One story suggests it was because a guy in the neighbourhood who couldn't pronounce 'Dermot' used to call him something that sounded like 'German'. Another story is that it came from some of his sketches imitating John Cleese doing his

German characters. (He had not yet met my and Bobby's mother, Susanne, who is German, but he always had a fascination with things German.) Whatever the original reason, the name still lives on among his friends from those days: I noticed when interviewing some of the guys from those days, they began talking about 'German' again.

Many insane things happened at the time; a lot of them, it would be fair to say, the product of mad nights out. Donagh's brother Eoin Morgan, who hadn't gone to college but was part of the gang, told me a while back about an incident which happened when the others were in college. He had rented a house in Ranelagh, which isn't a million miles away from UCD's Belfield campus. One night, he heard an almighty noise outside his house. He looked out to see some of the crowd from college coming down the road with a bulldozer, tearing up half the street. God knows what they did with it, though no doubt, they brought it back to where they'd found it and had a good laugh about it.

Dermot and his friends often got together in his home in Mount Merrion, just a short distance from Belfield, and had a whale of a time at impromptu gatherings and parties. There were all sorts of strange goings on, as people tried to gross each other out and do all they could to win in the continuous battles of wits which took place in those sessions. What was striking about all of this was that they had an ally in Holly, who seemed to revel in it all, apparently having taken a liking to Dermot's friends and their antics in her home. Maybe it made her feel young or something, and it was the kind of thing that wasn't wholly out of character. As Donagh recalls it: 'Mount Merrion... is where an awful lot of the madness ensued and Holly was leading the pack. She loved it.'

Although the social aspects of college life were a main focus for them, they obviously did a certain amount of study, although their level of study was probably based on what they reckoned would get them their required grades. 'Well, he *did* study... occasionally,' admits Fr Michael Paul Gallagher, his tutor and eventual friend, who presided over Dermot's funeral, 'but as with anything else, he did it with a certain sense of urgency... he was bright, you don't need to be told that.'

For all the fun and carry-on that they indulged in outside of lectures, Dermot and his friends often found a forum for debate, discussion and questioning in the more academic side of things, an atmosphere encouraged by staff. The first time Fr Michael Paul Gallagher encountered Dermot was during one of these open sessions that provided a formal structure to the sort of discussions that Dermot and his friends were having in the canteen. There was an English lecture every Saturday morning at ten, not everybody's favourite time of the week. Some of the time, it was delivered by Michael Paul who decided to reward those who turned up by having a more informal session afterwards. It was in this atmosphere halfway between a coffee morning and a seminar that he came to know Dermot as a frequent contributor to the open discussions.

College was also where he first came to explore seriously what he was, and was not, adept at. It was there that he began to test his capabilities as a performer. One of the most basic ways in which he went about doing this was to pose as a lecturer on the spur of the moment. He would pop into a lecture theatre where students were waiting for someone with even the vaguest sign of having a PhD to come and impart their knowledge. His friends, of course, egged him on to go out and perform as best he could. 'He used to spend his time in the theatres doing sketches, taking off the lecturers and so on. There was a gang of us around and whenever he'd have the urge to perform, he'd get up and give a lecture,' remembers Donagh.

He also used to perform on 'television' in the university residence in Roebuck Hall, where Donagh, Paddy and Robbie rented rooms and where others who lived locally, like Dermot and Karl Kelly, used to gather. He used a kitchen hatch in the flat as a 'television' through which to entertain and amuse all.

On one occasion he and Paddy Hehir went down to one of the commerce lectures which took place in the Arts Block and got up in front of the students, who assumed he was a genuine lecturer. According to Paddy, he stood up and with the utmost seriousness, turned to the class and said: 'Before I begin with this morning's lecture, I'd like to ask you all to join in this little piece myself and my colleagues have composed.' Then he broke into 'Magic Moments' with huge amounts of commitment, getting the commerce students to sing along. God knows what they made of the whole thing.

Lecture addresses, though, were not just encouraged by Dermot's friends. On one particular occasion in Dermot's third year, Fr Michael Paul was included in the conspiracy. Dermot approached him on the first day of the new college year and asked him if he was giving the Freshers their first English lecture. Michael Paul confirmed that he was. 'Gimme them,' Dermot demanded. So the two conspired to have Dermot go in and address the class posing as Michael Paul. That's when Dermot got his first priest's collar, from Michael Paul, one of the old-fashioned 'Roman' collars.

The plan was for Michael Paul to follow him into Theatre L and to denounce him as an impostor. However, Michael Paul went to the projection booth and let him go on for a while as Dermot prescribed two books for the course: 'The Bible — B-I-B-L-E — and Tottham's *Book of Cats*. The relationship between the two will become more apparent as the year progresses,' he promised them. Eventually, though, Michael Paul crept down from the projection booth, as the students began to suspect something was going on, and exposed Dermot, who scampered off.

College also led to adventures in the world of student drama, especially the kind that was full of scandal. Both Donagh and Paddy Hehir remember how, along with Dermot, they got roles in a play, probably *A Volunteer For Me*, by Harold Pinter, which caused a great deal of scandal at the time because it had male nudity. They were meant to play security guards, who 'beat up' a naked guy in bed. However, they decided they were method actors and got carried away with the role, interpreting it a little more roughly than they should have. But it was all good fun at the time.

Dermot always loved football in one form or another. In college, he and Paddy Hehir, who'd lived with Dermot in Mount Merrion for a year, joined the Foster team (named after a nearby road) of UCD's soccer super-league, an institution which still runs today. I think this venture was probably short-lived but it remained a happy memory for him — he was very eager that I should join up when I went to college. By that stage, I think he had already fostered his love for Ajax Amsterdam, who ruled European football at the time. He definitely went weak at the knees thinking of the likes of Cruyff and Neeskins and actually went off to Holland with his brother Paul, who was about sixteen at the time. It was also quite an adventure for them to explore what seemed to be such a far-off and wonderful place at that age: I imagine they had a great time.

One of the highlights of Dermot's time in UCD was the emergence of *Big Gom and the Imbeciles*, a piss-take of the many awful Country & Western showbands that were huge in Ireland at that time. (The name itself was a parody of one of the most famous showbands, *Big Tom and the Mainliners*.) Dermot was the main front-man, with Donagh, Paddy Hehir and Ak Kennedy also playing central parts. According to Paddy and Ak, they were the jokers on stage; the musicians of the ensemble were to be, well, musicians, acting in a 'professional' manner. When they auditioned musicians, Dermot and Paddy apparently stipulated that the keyboardist should be as 'webbed-handed' as possible. Eamonn Regan, a roommate of Paddy's, barely played a note and got in, having met the prerequisite of being very definitely a webbed-handed keyboardist. Dermot wanted a proper brass section but, the way things were, there was no chance of that happening so they opted for Paddy, Ak and Shay playing kazoos. It was just as good, if not better.

The show began with a few sketches and 'support' acts before the Big Gom band itself came on stage. The first sketch took the piss out of Samuel Beckett and provided a run-down on how to create your own Beckett play. Donagh Morgan and Paddy Hehir then performed a send-up of an old Irish *seannós* song, complete with a spittoon. Paddy provided the appropriate running commentary on poor Donagh, who sang a 'famous Bulgarian folk song, translated from the Russo-Czechoslovakian' which he claimed came from, 'a great 16th-century collector of songs and other sorts of shit'. From a surviving tape of the show, it seems that the initial jokes received a lukewarm reception, which no doubt sent a certain level of fear into the gang's minds. But as people got on the same wave-length as the band, they warmed to the surreal and raw humour being displayed. After the *seannós* singing, there was a jugband just for good measure, before *Big Gom* finally appeared and did their set. It went down a stormer.

Dermot pulled off fantastic mock Country & Western vocals in the thick Cavan accent he assumed , especially shining on such high points of the evening as the exceptionally sick ballad, *The Stain On My Father's Pyjamas.* As the concert progressed and the crowd got more and more into it, participating in every song, Dermot's voice was becoming more and more knackered, as he sang his heart, lungs, liver and other vital organs out. By the end he was lying on the stage completely exhausted, while the rest continued on. Paddy Hehir took over the singing for a while on a rowdy version of *The Hucklebuck.* The remainder of the concert saw Dermot return, his voice temporarily recovered, as they did a series of rock covers, featuring a very stomping version of a Gary Glitter track, which, amazingly, sounds better than the original on a recording I have of the gig. What's unmistakable, from listening to it, is the fact that the crowd were fully playing their part in making the whole thing the success it was, singing along and generally getting into the spirit of rowdiness that was coming from the act onstage. The musicians, too, got carried away and decided to have their own fun as well. At one stage in the show, on one of the more rocking songs, the guitarist's endless solos defeated a fairly shagged-out Dermot in gaining supremacy over the sound levels. At the end of the song, he conceded defeat: 'And the result is the lead guitarist won!'

Apparently Dermot was suffering from pneumonia at the time, but he kept performing to the end of the show. He was later taken to hospital with a collapsed lung.

Although the shows were a success, there were only a handful of *Big Gom* concerts, before they packed it in. Here, to give a flavour of them and their times, is the programme note from one of the last performances of a later re-incarnation of Big Gom:

☆

BIG GOM PRODUCTIONS

HOW IT ALL STARTED: In the autumn of 1972 German Morgan was released from prison, having served four-hundred-and-seventy-years of his twenty-five-year sentence for surprising a bull with a feather duster in the basement of Switzers. With this one crime a new phase had entered English — the "Bull in the China Shop".

Returning to UCD, he decided to wreak a terrible revenge on the society which had punished him for punishing the bull. He thought about taking his shoes off but realised the Geneva Convention had banned biological warfare. So first he tried putting large quantities of nail-varnish remover into the lemon meringue pie served in the Belfield restaurant. The consensus among the students was that the pie had improved — the move failed, humanity had triumphed. Demented German Morgan launched: Big Gom and the Imbeciles (uggh!) — gasp! Yes he had done his dirtiest so far!

The show started with a ventriloquist's dummy routine, ended with the German National Anthem, and in between came the special years ssshhh... the crowd were dosed with liberal helpings of Gentle Mother, a baroque piece written in County Monaghan, for a string quartet, not to mention drums, saxs, trumpets, car horns and the No. 1 Army Band. The crowd incidentally were given soap and towels as an inducement to get them to enter the chamber — the theatre that is. Encouraged by the fact that no one took legal action, *Big Gom and the Imbeciles* continued and this is their fourth production. Previous productions have included a Brian Clough commentary on the seduction of a female interviewer by his star player; and a garda patrol which tried to retrieve a bottom for a woman who had it pinched.

Personnel:

Dermot 'German' Morgan: Big Gom and the founder Imbecile.

Height	7' 4" Blonde, blue eyes
Hair	1' 1"
Eyes	right
Sex	yes please

Marion Casey: New Imbecile

Height	4', 4' 6", 4' 6", 4"
Hair	1' 2"
Eyes	left
Sex	are you kidding?

Paddy Courtney, Veteran Imbecile. Has a piece of shrapnel lodged in his bank account.

Height	7' 109"
Hair	artificial
Eyes	everything
Sex	Sundays, holidays, weekdays, tea-breaks, showers, baths and pavements.

Paul Morgan, New Imbecile — well an old one since birth in fact, first time in official capacity.

Height	occasionally
Hair	do you go to my lovely when you're alone in your bed?
Eyes	discreetly
Sex	between studies.

Olive Connolly, New Imbecile, does impression of rocking chair when running for buses.

Height	yes
Hair	yes
Eyes	yes
Sex	Are you kidding?

The Nun, (Deirdre Fortune)

Height	?
Hair	?
Eyes	?
Sex	novice

Joan Honneyman, Chris Nag, Finnola O'Sullivan, Brendan McManus (the first to sail a piano into Cuba despite US Navy).

A word on the band: guitars: Anthony Drennan, Martin McEvoy; bass: il Papa; drums: Brendan Farren; Electrician: Mick Malone.

☆

Big Gom was definitely one of the highlights of Dermot's shows in college but it wasn't the only one. He'd been learning how to play the bass and after a while was good enough to play in a band. When he got my brother Bobby his first bass, he told us of his own experience of not being able to get an amp, as his dad wouldn't buy him one and he couldn't afford one himself. As a result he found himself blowing the guts out of many a radio. *Johnny and the Gents* was the product of his faithful hours of practise and it meant that those radios weren't obliterated in vain. He was *Johnny*, and the *Gents* included Liam Redmond and Paddy Courtney.

Their attitude was that if Bob Geldof and the Boomtown Rats could do, then so could they. They played a few gigs, appeared at a few dances and the like, and went on for a while. Dermot and Pat Finn did the promotional and management work for the group — not the last of their business endeavours together.

College, however, was coming to an end. After all the fun, the performances and the general madness, Dermot went on to complete and pass his exams, getting his BA — the goal of his studies — in 1974, the year his father died. He'd got his education and now he had to go off into the real world.

I'd say that in his years in college Dermot learned a few things about himself and his ambitions for life. He liked to perform, be it entertaining his friends through the kitchen hatch 'television' in Roebuck Hall, pretending to be a teacher in the lecture theatres of UCD, or performing in Theatre L, the venue of his experiences with *Big Gom and the Imbeciles*. It got something going in his system, something that clicked for him in such environments.

After he left UCD *Big Gom* and all the other performances he had done there became just a memory. That said, it was a memory he shared with us — one of those things you grew up knowing about: Daddy was in UCD and he did something called *Big Gom*. Not that college was totally divorced from his life afterwards. When I got my place in UCD, he told me how he and some of his friends, such as Pat Finn, went back to college for Freshers' Week for several years after they had left to check out what was going on there and to relive their glory days.

Sad old boys, as he used to say.

CAN I HAVE YOUR ATTENTION PLEASE?

After leaving college, Dermot entered that strange and scary place we call the Jobs Market. He already had an array of summer and part-time jobs behind him by then, including a stint on the trawlers and another working in the UCD canteen. But he needed something a lot more long-term now. He wanted to do what he always wanted to do — write and perform —but he needed to keep himself and, later, a family as well. So he became a teacher, as did some of his friends, studying for and getting his Higher Diploma in Education, which qualified him as a secondary-school teacher. Teaching as such meant another type of performance, which, as with other comedians who began in the same profession, allowed him to get used to levelling with the hecklers and messers in the classroom: the best place to learn how to kill the heckling.

He went on to teach in a number of places, varying from Stillorgan Senior college, a kind of polytechnic, to St Michael's in Ballsbridge, a vaguely upper-class school run by a religious order, after he had completed a state-sponsored conversion course to train secondary teachers as primary teachers. He continued at the latter school as a substitute teacher until he had to make the choice between teaching and his career as a performer. In between these schools, he worked in the Royal Dublin Society in the Superintendent's office for a while.

All the time he was working, though, Dermot continued to write sketches and jot down ideas he had for shows; to develop himself as the performer he really wanted to be. He attempted to organise some gigs for himself, but wanting to become a stand-up comedian in the Ireland of the 1970s was not as easy as it might sound. At that time, it was like going on a very, very lonely wagon train over an untamed prairie. There wasn't really much available in the way of a comedy circuit in the modern sense of the phrase, nor was there much in the way of 'alternative' comedy either. Dermot was one of the pioneers, as Ardal O'Hanlon, who himself started out as a stand-up, noticed about him:

> I think certainly in the ten years before I started, and I started in 1988 or thereabouts, he was the only representative of that kind of alternative type of comedy in Ireland. In that sense he was a maverick who cropped up from time to time on different TV shows with different characters and lampoons, and I was very aware of his presence.

What did exist, however, was the cabaret circuit, referred to by Dermot's friend Pat Finn as 'the chicken-and-chips circuit', where stand-up was dominated by comedians of the old school telling mother-in-law jokes and that type of thing. Dermot's humour was at the polar opposite of that tradition of comedy. It wasn't his cup of tea at all — he had his mind focussed on doing something a lot different. His humour was more akin to the likes of Billy Connolly or any of the early alternative comics in Britain, but because Ireland didn't have anything like this at the time, he suffered for it in those initial attempts at stand-up. As Pat described in his foreword to the book, it was a tough time, appearing in working men's clubs where the audience showed a total lack of interest in his act. It's almost like he entered the real world of comedy, which was a lot harsher than his experiences in college. 'In college we knew all the in-jokes and stuff,' explains Paddy Hehir who, along with some other of Dermot's friends, went to some of those initial and less successful gigs.

There was a sense that what he was trying to do would be hard in the circumstances in which he had to work. But that wasn't going to deter him in any way: if anything, he was probably fuelled by the challenge of doing something so innovative.

Many of his friends from that time make the point that he listened to any number of comedians in order to find inspiration — ways of improving and refining his own act and harnessing his own inherent humour in the best way possible. Robbie O'Connell singles out Monty Python as the great marker for Dermot, proving to him that what he wanted to do was possible. Python was definitely one of his absolute favourites as Bobby and I discovered quite early on in our lives, as he had a sense of surreal madness similar to Dermot, and that reflected in Dermot's humour.

Paddy remembers Dermot listening to any stand-up comedian — good, bad, ugly or indifferent — that would help him expand and refine his act. As well as the strong influence of Monty Python, he was also influenced in certain ways by the likes of Billy Connolly, Woody Allen and even Lenny Bruce, whose humour was, to be honest, radically different to Dermot's. In fact, Dermot built up a great collection of comedy records by the people I've mentioned among others.

As time went by, he got into doing more and more gigs. He played in Carrick-on-Suir in Tinvale Hotel, which is owned by his friend Robbie O'Connell's family, on several occasions from the beginning of his stand-up career. In Dublin, he played here, there and everywhere and was a resident in the Suffolk House in Dublin's city centre for a time. One of the strangest venues, though, was in the Oscar Theatre in Sandymount, Dublin where he shared the bill with a stripper and the female impersonator, Alan Amsby, aka Mr Pussy. Dermot did the bulk of his routine there as Father Trendy, the hip priest; apparently, that billing began with the stripper coming out on the stage naked and shouting, 'Can I have your attention please!'

Another part of Dermot's act in those days was to bring a suitcase onto the stage with him. He opened it up to produce a friend of his, Brendan McManus, dressed in a sailor suit, pretending to be a ventriloquist's dummy.

Around that time broadcaster Mike Murphy was becoming increasingly aware of Dermot and his work. He used to have an early morning radio show which was less serious than the news and current affairs programmes that surrounded it. Dermot used to send him letters as Father Trendy, which Mike found incredibly funny and would read on air. Then, Mike Murphy was given his own television show *The Live Mike*. It soon became apparent to those working on it that they could make use of Dermot's talents.

The four years or so of *The Live Mike* were extremely fruitful for Dermot, who popped up in different guises throughout the show. There was his mad GAA fanatic who, wielding a hurley stick, vented his fury at how the show and the media in general treated traditional rural values. And there was Father Trendy, the hip priest who was totally in touch with the youth of the day and made no secret of how 'with it' he was in his 'sermons'. Father Trendy, the latest in the series of incarnations of the hip priest that he had been doing since the mock lectures in Belfield, became the character Dermot was best known for in the late 1970s and early 1980s. Father Trendy was not based on any one person but was a caricature of the many 'trendy', media-friendly, priests who emerged at that time, the kind who appeared on the nightly 'God slot' on television and used an approach which they thought to be 'with-it'. I've always suspected that Michael Paul Gallagher, Dermot's old lecturer and friend from college, has a tendency towards this type of performance; I noticed this again at Dermot's funeral, and grinned to myself.

The experience Dermot got from doing *The Live Mike* was invaluable to his development. He was able to work with some of the top people around at the time, including Mike Murphy himself, Twink, and Fran Dempsey. He also had the chance to work with other writers who shared similar outlooks on comedy such as Eanna Brophy and Paddy Murray. And he also learned a lot about the ways of television: for instance, the writers of the comedy sketches for the show, Dermot, Eanna and Paddy, used to have regular meetings with the wider programme team. The aforementioned three would be at one end of the table laughing over their scripts. At the other end would be others, some of who didn't see anything funny. So the writers would have to explain the scripts, a procedure that became known among them as the 'Defend Your Script' ritual.

Between the stand-up and the television work, things were beginning to come together for Dermot.

THE SERMONS OF
FATHER TRENDY

FOREWORD

You know, the first thing I'd like to say about my work as a trendy priest is that it is vital in this modern world of ours to be *with-it.*

This may puzzle some older readers, but I ask you, what is the alternative to being with-it? And you know, when you think about it, you realise the answer can only be: being without-it. I don't need to comment on this possibility. It would be a situation which nobody would welcome.

And so, if my sermons were going to speak to today's world, and in particular today's youth, I realised that I would have to go out and immerse myself in the world of Pop Music and Show Business, in order that I might be able to speak the language of today, Baby. You see what I mean — the fact that I can quite comfortably throw in the word "Baby" at the end of a sentence helps me immeasurably in getting my message across.

It's all about communicating. I remember talking to a group of young people one evening at the local community centre, and they appeared to me to be — how shall I say — a little disinterested in what I was saying. There were a few tell-tale signs which indicated this. Nothing terribly obvious, just small little things the youth were doing, which betrayed a slight apathy towards my message. Some of them seemed to be concentrating on their acne problem, assisting each other in the search for pimples which required first-aid attention. Others were engrossed in combing their hair, while still others were enthusiastically practising their woodwork on the desks in the centre.

Don't get me wrong — I *like* to see young people expressing themselves in every medium possible, even the community centre tables. But I also realised that I needed to make my sermons a little more interesting.

I was talking, as it happened, about the lives of the saints. I asked who was the patron saint of travellers. One boy interrupted to say that he had never known that Thomas Cook was a saint. I laughed. It was a harmless little quip, a little bit of fun.

The answer to my next question shook me a bit, I must confess. I asked to whom would they pray to if they had lost something. One little boy, about nineteen, put his hand up at the back. (I think this boy was the life-saving instructor, because heretofore he had, for the duration of my little chat, been showing the girl beside him how to revive someone with mouth-to-mouth resuscitation. Personally, I was surprised how long it takes to revive someone in this manner.) Anyway, he pointed out that if the lost item or items had been insured there would be no need to pray to any saint. This really made me think just how materialistic our world today has become.

How was I to speak meaningfully to these young people? I went out immediately and had a new set of clerical "gear" made in black satin. I decided to make the fullest use of modern media to get my message across. And of course I decided to make the odd little joke. We all need to smile, don't we? Of course we do.

Actually, at that little youth group meeting at which I spoke of the saints, several of the "lads" were very amusing about the roles of saints. One particularly wild boy asked me if I knew who the patron saint of underwear was. Before I had time to react, he took a small item of ladies' lingerie, and holding up the label on it, surmised that it might in fact be Saint Michael. A certain amount of good-natured barracking ensued until the boy (let's call him Tony) informed another boy (let's call him Joe) that the underwear belonged to his sister.

At this the barracking became less good-natured. Joe strenuously denied the suggestion. I guess that you could say that tempers *frayed*, and between the pulling and the pushing, so did the underwear! It showed me how volatile the young people can be. It was quite some time (and many bingo sessions) later that we raised the money to re-build the centre.

So, as you see, it was essential that I learn to speak the language of the young people today. I tried to get them to see that God is "groovy" and religion is a "cool vibe". At first I found it hard to learn this lingo, but I looked on myself as a kind of missionary trying to convert a lost tribe. Instead of going down the Amazon, I was going into a world of young people — a world with all the problems of drugs, sex and drink.

I had to learn the strange ways of this tribe, in order to become accepted by them. OK, so I had to learn to be "groovy". I had to know what I was talking about. If a young person came to me and asked me about contraceptives, I had to be able to honestly say: "No, they are not cool, man." I had to be able to say: "Listen, man, I've tried condoms, and I don't know how any person young or old can stand the taste of them." I had to be able to say: "That's not where it's at, head."

We're in a crazy old world, and we've got to respond to its special challenges. I remember the first time I spoke in the modern way of speaking to my Bishop. I was discussing a marathon breath-holding competition for charity, and without thinking I replied to a particular point by saying: "I couldn't agree with you there, Your Grace, man." He was shocked, but I pointed out to him that "Man" is a great way of constantly reminding ourselves of our humanity. After all, we are not fish, or elephants, or field mice, or antelopes, or armadillos, but *MAN:* i.e. Men and Women. And I think he took this point without too much rancour, even if he did transfer me to candle-lighting and bell-ringing for a few months.

That spell of bell-ringing didn't hurt me at all. I had a lot of time to think during those lonely mornings in the belfry. The other curates in the parish used to make a little joke about me eventually getting bats in my belfry, but I learned a lot there. As I would rise and fall, hanging on the end of the rope, I would think how this experience mirrored life itself... a series of ups-and-downs.

There were times during my solitary tolling at those bells when I would feel angry, thinking that I was being treated like Quasimodo, but then I realised that being Quasimodo is a state of mind, a state of ugliness. Only anger can turn me into a Quasimodo, because it makes me get my back up.

Such were the reflections which filled my mind during that time. Those bells woke me up... well, indeed, it would be very hard to stay asleep with them... they became like the vast bells on God's huge telephone to me.

Actually I must tell you of an amusing little anecdote that a friend of mine, a curate in an inner-city parish was telling me. He was saying that once a year they hold a Mass for ex-boxers. Unfortunately there was a little mishap at the first of the Masses. On that occasion, when the altar boy rang the bells the entire congregation proceeded to go three rounds with the person next to them!

The bells naturally put matrimony into my mind on occasions. They reminded me of the first wedding I performed. It was on the Missions. For that particular tribe, it was their first Christian wedding. There was naturally some confusion, and indeed when the ring was produced the young groom tried to put it through his bride's nose.

There was also some acrimony over the term "best man", which expression rankled badly with the groom to the extent that various challenges were issued to contest this particular appellation. I smile now when I think of those wonderful days, with the little mishaps and misunderstandings as those wonderful people acquired Christian culture. But that particular day will always stand out for the laughter and merriment and good humour with which the groom's family accepted my explanation of the best man's role. And I may say that once they understood the meaning of the expression "best man", they laughed openly and, without further delay or bad feeling, cut him down immediately.

I always think that the use of a ring at the marriage ceremony is particularly apt, because in some sense marriage is a bit of a circus. There are certain acts that must be performed if the young couple are to enjoy life together. Together they may have to know some of the skills of a circus.

It could happen, for example, that the husband might come home a bit late for tea some evening, slightly under the weather, and the wife knows the mood is not too good, and yet she feels she must say something. At times like that, she must feel she is walking a bit of a tightrope. The husband by the same token must acquire the skills of the lion-tamer... he must learn not only *how* to draw the lion but *where* to draw it.

The wife can justly expect her husband to be the Strongman when it comes to putting out the bins each week, et cetera. But I must say that he would have grounds for an annulment if she transpired to be a bearded lady! (a little joke does no harm.)

Yes, marriage is a bit of a circus, there are spills and thrills, and you have to learn that like any circus, you must pay the price. What I would say is, enjoy the circus, but don't start clowning around, for if you do you will, like the trapeze artist, inevitably be caught in the act.

I guess you could say that it was my time hanging out of the bell rope which, in a very real sense, turned me into a Swinging Priest. It was a great experience, even if it left my hearing slightly impaired.

Naturally, after all that, I am glad of the opportunity to go on television and give sermons to so many, and I hope they get the message across to you in the comfort of your own sitting-rooms. I hope you all know that, when the red light on the camera comes on, and I peer into that lens, I'm trying to reach out and be there in your living room, on the sofa, beside each and every one of you, so that we could have a brief little chat, for an hour or two about Life and Religion, and the World, and Football, and so on...

The television is my pulpit. I hope you'll all "turn on" to religion.

Hell's Angel

Life's a motorbike and you might as well get up on it, grab it by the handlebars and see if you can get a kick out of it. But as you speed along don't forget the passenger on the back – your Guardian Angel. But you've got to ask yourself:

"Am I following the road signs, and am I wearing the crash helmet, the crash helmet which is prayer?"

Fill up your tank with religion so you don't become a Hell's Angel. Yes, life is a motorbike, in that sometimes we may feel we are coasting along on a Triumph, and yet maybe our religion demands a BMW – a Bit More Work.

The Big Match

Over the weekend the big talking point for most people was the Big Match. Who's going to win the big match? I couldn't help asking myself, What about the really Big Match? The one we all play, against Devils United, Lucifer Athletic, Hell FC?

We're all playing for Christian Rovers, or are we? When the Devil floats a tempting ball into your defence, will you use your head? Will you take up that cross? Will you send that sin all the way back to his part of the field? Yes, the question is, are you a good player for God?

Maybe, lads, when you go to a party you start making passes, and I don't mean the Liam Brady type of pass. And maybe after the party you come home and have a disagreement with your wife. Do you become a strike 'er?

And girls, what about you? Do you realise that parties often provide some of the toughest matches against the Devil. Remember how easy it is to become a little forward.

There are two options in life, one simple, one divine. I hope you'll do like Terry Neill and pick the Devine.

The Bus Service

Space travel is surely one of the miracles (no offence, Lord, ha, ha!) of the twentieth century. But you know there is another form of travel which never fails to amaze me. *Bus* travel. Yes, this more humble everyday form of transport is in itself a source of wonder, a minor miracle. We even hear the hardy commuter make the remark: "It will be a bloody miracle if the bus comes." And indeed even I myself have been tempted to think of space on our buses... if only we had a little more of it. I'm sure that that is a thought which crosses most peoples' minds from time to time. *If only we had more space on this bus.* And indeed, I'm sure they often think: *If only we had a bus.* Well, not to worry, that's one of those things.

I always like to think that CIE bring us a bit more into contact with religion. They give us pause for thought. Sometimes they give us very long pauses for thought, and let's be honest, one can think and pray as well at a bus stop as anywhere else. Waiting for a bus can bring into focus the meaning of the concept of *eternity,* sometimes we seem to be afforded the reality of eternity. So you see buses have a very important role in our lives — a very important role in our lives — a very important spiritual role. They teach us humility. OK, we all tend to forget how relatively small we are in the universe, we tend to think we are important, but when a bus sails by leaving you standing there, you realise that not only will the world not stop for you but sometimes not even your common or garden bus will stop for you.

I sometimes tend to think of life as a sort of bus journey. Life itself is akin to a bus. We're all travelling together, hurtling along to our destination and along the way there are going to be bumps. Yes, bumps, and why not? Did we really expect it to be a smooth trip? And life is equally full of disappointments. Maybe you'd like to have got off at a particular stop. OK, the driver says *No!* Like God he controls our destiny. God is the driver, and indeed sometimes bus drivers tend to think of themselves in God's role. And why not? They are teaching us important lessons.

Yes, life may be studied on a bus. Often I'm reminded of Noah's Ark from the Old Testament, because the bus passengers are travelling in twos. And, let's be honest, some Saturday nights you see the odd boy and girl behaving like a pair of animals. It saddens me that some lads tend to treat their girlfriends as passengers. She puts out her hand to try and stop him but he just keeps on going. He assumes that she is a full-fare passenger and wants to go all the way!

At times like that I would ask girls to respond by behaving like the good conductor and telling him where to get off.

Yes, for me buses are a religious experience. And what do those letters CIE say to me? They say: Christ Is Everywhere.

That's just the ticket!

The Clothing Department

Little Tom once asked me to define religion. I was hard put to give him an answer but after some thought I replied, "Imagine that you only have one pair of trousers," I said. "They are a bit tight, a hard to get into... but they're the only ones you've got. That's what religion is like. It's like a pair of trousers. It may not be always comfortable. There'll be times when we find it hard to wear, when we really start to feel the pinch. Nonetheless, we can't just discard it there and then in the street!

"There'll be times when we feel it is strangling us... those are the times when we must take a deep breath and keep on.

"Faith is the zip which holds religion together. Often we must look and check is our faith slipping, if we are letting it run down. That is something we must all go through. That does not mean we should unduly worry, because religion by its very nature is hard to button down."

"That's all very well said for little Tommy, but what about me?" said Sheila. "I don't wear trousers. How am I to know what religion is?" I knew this would be more difficult, but I knew it also had to be faced up to. I told Tornmy to go and kick the football around. Gently I took Sheila aside and said:

"Sheila, there is only one way I can describe religion for a girl. It's a bra." She looked a bit shocked for a moment or two, but I just smiled and told her not to be alarmed.

"You see Sheila," I said, "religion is what gives one uplift in this troubled world of ours. It's what helps us get ourselves together. It helps us carry our burdens through life, and life has its fair share of troubles. There'll be times, sure, when we'll all come up against the knockers... the ones who want to stand in our way. Those are the times when we turn to religion, when we 'cross our hearts' in the spiritual sense. We won't be perfect. We all make our fair share of boobs, when our faith is a bit wobbly, but that's the very time we must put our best foot forward and hang in there."

Do you know that after my simple but effective little explanation, Tommy and Sheila walked away from me, and they were so moved that tears were rolling down their cheeks!

The Head Barman

The following words do not concern most people in Ireland. They are addressed to a very small minority of people – probably only one or two percent. I am speaking to that little known group of people who take alcohol once in a while, and so I have tried to put this in language, which they will understand.

Because for the man or woman who spends his time in the bar, it is sometimes hard to present a true view of the world outside, and especially difficult to explain about religious matters. For instance, Heaven is exceptionally hard to conceive of when you are already totally happy on your bar stool.

Firstly let me say to drinkers that prayer has some similarities to drinking, in that for some it is also a religious practice. That's what true religious practice means — going to the church to pray as often and as seriously as drinking, even.

Life itself can be justly compared to an evening in a pub. We are only given a certain amount of time. God is the Head Barman. He is watching your behaviour, and when it comes to Closing Time he'll decide whether you should be admitted to that big Pub in the Sky or whether you should be barred.

Human nature is as diverse as the drinks in a public house. Some of us can be like bad pints – full of ourselves, but we don't have very much up there in the "head". Some of us take a long time to settle.

When it comes to real religious feeling, maybe we've gone a little flat. Maybe our faith is a little 'short". Maybe we confine ourselves to "double" thinking. Let's try to remember that life is not all "Black and White". Perhaps our "Spirit" needs to mature.

We are all pints on God's counter, and God wants to pull those pints for Himself, if only you will let him. The pint I want to make is that your faith must be a stout one if you want to end up with a Harp.

The Incredible Hulk

Not too long ago I came home to the presbytery — my pad — tired or as they say down at the youth club "knackered" from a hard day's priestly duties; slaving over a hot altar — if you will. I sat down to watch the television and what should appear on the screen but a programme entitled *The Incredible Hulk*. I nodded my head sadly as I realised the all pervading influence of that adjective today... INCREDIBLE. We just don't have enough belief in this modern world of ours... we believe so little and I am not just talking about people who don't believe in God. People who refuse to believe in all sorts of things... they are filled with doubt and scepticism. I have a hunch that there are people who don't believe the sun will rise in the morning. They are probably those who don't even believe the four seasons will follow each other year in year out — it's crazy absolutely crazy — the next thing people will start to question whether the bus is going to arrive. There just isn't enough belief about.

I felt an immediate sense of compassion and understanding for this "Incredible" Hulk. To myself I muttered quietly 'I believe you'. Imagine his frustration in trying to gain acceptance in the community when people insist on calling him 'incredible'... Let's be quite clear about this: changing a skinny but brilliant medical scientist and researcher into a seven-foot square green giant who bursts his clothes is no mean trick. It is a great talent and gift. I know lads who get invited to parties for less.

What does the Hulk have to do to become credible? Surely growing two-hundred percent in size and weight and turning green is enough to warrant some attention... Is this explosion not some cry for help and notice? Why do they insist on 'incredible'? What do they then think is happening?

"Oh there goes David having one of his turns" or "David looks a little sickly tonight... he's positively green."

From a moral point of view I commend the programme makers for the tasteful way they ensure that only his shirt and the ends of his trousers burst. Seemingly the waistband of his trousers is more resilient. We don't want too much realism do we?

"Thank God" I often say to my housekeeper Ingrid, "that the Hulk is a man – I'm sure if it was a women who burst her blouse like that we'd be scandalised. Ha, ha." Though doubtless Women's Libbers will feel that there should be an Incredible Hulkesse. Mind you I've seen some photographs of Raquel Welch and other actresses who appear to be bursting out of their clothes!!!!

But seriously though, the Hulk symbolises the pent-up anger and rage which we all have within us but which we must learn to control. I sometimes feel tempted to say to the Hulk when he storms through a wall "Now, now, temper, temper." or "Don't you ever think of trying the door first?" I suppose that type of comment is beside the point though. I do think however that the Hulk should teach lads in particular not to lose their tempers and to be careful not to destroy the clothes which Mammy and Daddy have worked so hard to put on your back.

Granted, it's only a television fiction but if you imagine if the Hulk were a real person — think of his poor mother — her heart would be broken forever mending his shirts and sewing buttons back on them.

On deeper reflection let's remember that the Hulk is basically a good guy (and may I say if only we could discover an Irish grandmother in his ancestry — the answer to Ireland's perennial problem of who should partner Moss Keane in the second row). His anger is usually triggered by some wrong or injustice, which he sees committed. I say

"Hear, Hear" to that... we should all be bursting with indignation and anger at the injustice and wrong doing... but even so the most valuable lesson we can learn from the Hulk is that while we may get mad at something – keep your shirt on.

The Rolls Royce

Outside a Dublin hotel one night I saw a Rolls parked. It made me think wouldn't it be nice if we all had Rolls. And then I thought but we all do have Rolls or should I say roles — which we must fulfil.

People often refer to the road of life, and there's no doubt that we are all vehicles on that road. Sitting behind a young man at a parish disco one night I couldn't but help hear them discussing what I assumed was a car. One lad said that 'she was fast' and that 'she was an automatic'. Sadly I discovered it was not a car they spoke of. But it reinforced in my mind the similarity between human beings and cars.

We've got to know the direction we're going in and when to apply the brakes if we are to avoid the 'clutch' of the Devil.

When we go to church we should, like the good driver, be in the right gear, but not 'tanked up to the top' like some of the lads who come to evening Mass directly from the local 'filling station'.

That Rolls I spoke of earlier had a dinted front wing. It reminded me of the bad angels... they too had their wings clipped!

Drive carefully.

The Soccer Team

I remember one day being at Mass in the seminary, and all the other lads around me had their missals, but one subdeacon only had an Irish International match programme. A bishop told him to put it away, and afterwards he was brought up before the Cardinal, who asked him, "Why were you reading a programme in church, son?" And so I began to tell my tale:

"You see, Your Eminence, when I look at the Number One, I think of God, and the Number One is also the goal-keeper, ever-vigilant and trying to keep out the ball, just as we should be guarding our souls against sin. We should be soul-keepers.

"Then I see Number Two – John Devine, who reminds me that we should all try in a sense to be more divine. Then I see Ahsley Grimes, left back, and I think of that sixpence from Mammy's purse — I took it, but then I thought it was better-left back.

"Then I see the midfield trio, Gerry Daly, Tony Grealish and Liam Brady, and I think of the three wise men, and like the three wise men they had to follow a star — Johnny Giles.

"I think of the way after a hard tackle the coach gives them the magic sponge, like the Good Samaritan who stopped along the Damascus highway — which reminds me of another Heighway: Steve Heighway.

"Then we come to Frank Stapleton, Number Nine, which reminds me of the nine ungrateful lepers, and I think of how Frank can fairly lep to head the ball himself. And when he rises thus he reminds me of the words of the greatest manager of all. "Take Up Thy Cross." Frank not only takes up his cross, but he scores from it.

"And then we come to Johnny Giles, and I think of the virtue of purity. Girls, when you go to the disco, is there a bit of the Johnny Giles about you? Are you a little forward?"

So the Cardinal told me to go free... And friends, this story is true. I know. I was that boy.

The Space Programme

Not so long ago I was at a practice for a Folk Mass. There were many young people there, each with a prayer book and a Woolworth's guitar. We sang many songs – songs of young people – yes, even pop songs. We sang songs like "You've Got a Friend" (I think we all know who that friend is – we need look no further than heaven). We sang a few more song like "Sing A Song", "All You Need Is Love" and a little pop song I wrote myself specially for Folk Masses called "Let's All Jive For Jesus!" I have written one or two other little numbers, which I hope in their own humble and modest way, may just get The Message across, e.g. "the Bible Beat" a song I wrote to emphasise that the name *Peter* was given to the Church's own *Rock*... the rock on which the Church was formed... to stress the meaning and value of Peter as the first "Rock" of all, I have re-written such titles as "Jailhouse Peter", "Peter around the Clock", "Peter and Roll Music" etc.

I find that young people are quite surprised by the paraphrases... that can't be bad, can it?

I have said earlier that Pop or Rock (Peter) music is a language of its own. I noticed how one of the young lads at the Folk Mass practice who kindly donates his time to our group is himself a member of a local punk group. He called me "Head" (actually he had enough respect to say "Father Head") and sometimes "Man"... which I think is nice as it points to my, and indeed all, our humanity. Sometimes he would call me "Baby" (Father Baby): this I thought stresses the words of Our Lord that we must all become as children once again. I saw that young man exercising great care, even love, for his fellow guitarist. He turned to one girl beside him and asked her if she was cool. I thought that was

Dermot's parents Holly and Donnchadh at a dinner dance in the late 50s. Note Donnchadh's film star appearance.

Dermot (left) with Holly, Denise and Paul on the day of Paul's communion, c. 1965.

Dermot with his sister Ruth and Bran the dog, c. 1955

Dermot and his father, c. 1958

Robbie O'Connell's last night in Ireland, Roebuck Hall, early 70s. Note Dermot in the hatch (his television). Clockwise (from top) Donagh Morgan, Dermot, Robbie O'Connell, Clare Kelly, Karl Kelly, Paddy Hehir.

The 'Brian Wilson' pose, late 1960s

Looking moody with his first bass guitar in the garden at Mount Merrion, late 1960s

Big Gom and the Imbeciles in action,
Theatre L, UCD, 1972.

Johnny and the Gents pose for a publicity shot, early 70s.

Oh, Father!

From being a "Father" actor back to being a Daddy, that's the position "Fr. Brian Trendy" (alias Dermot Morgan) finds himself in this week, after his wife Susanne (28) had given birth to an 8lb. 8 ozs. baby boy at St. Colmcille's Hospital, Loughlinstown. Meeting the new addition to the family at the hospital this morning was the Morgan's 17½-month-old son, Don.
—Picture Tony Reddy.

AIR HOLIDAY OUTLOOK STILL BLEA

IT COULD be another disaster weekend for Irish holidaymakers booked for Europe's sun

Jobless to top

Dermot posing as 'Fr Trendy' becomes a daddy for the second time. This photo appeared in the *Evening Herald* after Bobby's birth.

'Doug' and 'Dinsdale' working on Dermot's hangover.

Three men in a tub. Bobby (left), Don and Dermot, 1983.

'Play that funky music...' Don and Dermot in the front garden of Mount Merrion, 1982.

Gumbies on tour, Ellman, 1992.
(from left) Bobby, Dermot and Don.

'I love working for...'
On a drill in Dingle, Co. Kerry 1992.

'The gurriers', in our front garden, 1983.

Don (top), Dermot and Bobby, 1982.

Dermot's favourite photo of himself with youngest son Ben, 1994.

A young frequent flyer: Ben regularly travelled between London and Dublin with his dad, during the shooting of *Father Ted*.

Ben and his dad take a stroll.

Ben and Dermot on the beach.

truly loving, truly considerate, truly caring. He wanted to know if his fellow man, or woman as it was in this particular instance, was warm enough or a little chilly or whatever. And they call these young people punks???

He then asked her if she was in anyway hungry. "Have you any bread, Mary Baby?" She hadn't. And then he offered to take her back and share his Sunday dinner with her. "C'mon back to my pad, I've got a joint!" Isn't this what life should be all about, sharing everything from the Sunday dinner or whatever? That's what we should dig. Those are the "vibes."

That boy spoke of being "spaced out", wanting to get spaced out. Naturally the room was quite crowded and I wanted myself to give everyone a little more room. The implications of *spaced out* as an expression are worth considering. I sometimes watch *Star Trek*. I guess my favourite character is Dr. Spock. One young lad tried to persuade me that Dr. Spock is an ex-Christian Brothers Boy. I enquired how he had got the information or what made him so certain. I was told that the pointed ears are a telltale sign of an ex-CB's boy; they tend to have ears like that as a result of long years of the Brothers' principle method of gaining a pupil's attention. Well, I'm sure that was just a little joke. Dr. Spock with his highbrow tones sounds to me more like a Jesuit lad, probably Mungret or Clongowes. Ha, ha.

In many ways, however, there are serious things that *Star Trek* can teach us. Things we should peruse. Couldn't we all do with "Enterprise' in our lives? Wouldn't that transport us to a higher life? Couldn't we use a bit more joy in our world? A smile or two? Isn't it time that we "beamed up" at our neighbours, once in a while?

The World

We were talking about the world. It's a subject, which I feel we are all, at least in some sense, bound to have in common, I hope. You know it's all the rage these days to say how small the world has become; how the world has shrunk, thanks to modern communications and jet-age travel. I wonder. I don't think we should lose sight of fact that notwithstanding jet aeroplanes, rockets, and space shuttles and what have you, the world is still *big*. I suppose you could say that discussions on the size of the world have broken down into two schools of thought. Those who say that the world is *big* and those who say it is *small*.

I'm afraid I'll have to nail my colours to the mast on this one, and come out in favour of the contention that the world is *big*. Indeed my opponents in this philosophical tussle say I should nail – not my colours – but my collar to the mast on this issue. Ha, ha. This is in all the nature of good-humoured banter which philosophers and theologians exchange with opponents. There is no acrimony about it – it's all part of a good day's thinking. In fact some philosophical opponents of mine once remarked that not only should my collar be nailed to the mast but that I should be in it at time. Ha, ha, ha. But I'm sure they didn't mean it.

So, to sum up my line of thinking so far on this subject in a way which I feel everyone can grasp: the world is big. And to those who try to minimise its size and volume and say it's small – can I just say, if it's so small thanks to the telephone and the jet – how would they like it if it dropped on their toe? Ha, ha, you see? It's all very well to knock the world which God created (without, I might add, the help of the first-time owner's building grant). My guess is that they would not be quite so smart in that event. My guess is that it's easy to say how small the world is but that not only would they not like it dropped on their foot, nor yet a jet, but that they would not savour even dropping a mere telephone on their foot. Sure, some of the witty proponents of a small world have said that this is so merely because it's so difficult to get a phone in the first place, let alone replace the one you drop on your foot in spurious experiments conducted in relation to ascertaining the dimensions of the world. Anyhow I think we can all take it for certain that the world is big. Think of the vastness of it. Think of all the drops of water in the great oceans of the world. Think of all the grains of sand in her deserts. Think of all the houses in Tallaght.

And they try to say the world is small!

One thing I have noticed about the world in my travels is its countries. Different countries, each with its own people: Ireland the Irish, Sweden the Swedes and so on. I think we should respect this distinctiveness. For if it were not there we would not know what to expect when we went there. We might find that Russia was Spanish for example. This would be crazy, wouldn't it? Think of how difficult it would make life for travel agents, for openers. Maybe after a hard year Daddy and Mammy decide to take us all to a Spanish resort in November and we might end up with our suntan lotion and bathing gear in Leningrad. We'd look silly, wouldn't we — in our sawn-off denim shorts and "I Shot JR" t-shirts strolling around in six inches of snow.

We might find the capital of Holland was Kampala, that they spoke Polish in Mexico and the great Trans-Amazon Highway by-passed Naas, which of course it does in sense.

So it's nice therefore to know which country is which. It helps us to recognise the world. And after all if the world were one big country it would be boring, I think. That's not to say that we shouldn't all learn from each other and try to become closer. My travels have given me pause for thought over the years. I have put down below a few of the things I have seen and my reflections on them:

Sweden

Saunas are fine. It's important for all to let off a little steam once in a while, but should we sit around naked in it?

Spain

There's a bit of the matador in us all. We like to side-step our problems, but sooner or later we're going to slip and then we'll find there's a lot of bull in us as well.

Holland

Sometimes like Holland we feel a little flat and in the dikes of our minds there is a gap which we can't quite put a finger on... and still like the little Dutch boy we've got to keep plugging away.

Germany

I saw someone in West Berlin shouting across to a relative in East Berlin. You know it reminded me of praying... our message gets through even though we can't see Him and sometimes it feels like we're talking to a wall. I saw the Wall, the sentries in their towers and the inevitable wire everywhere. You know the wire reminded me of a politician's speech; it was guarded, it went on and on, plenty of barbs in it and always sitting squarely on the fence.

Yes, the world is big, diverse , but I think of it as the globe you had in the school classroom; you can learn from it and don't be afraid to give it a whirl.

FOOTBALL AND FATHERHOOD

by Susanne Morgan

I first met Dermot when he was working in the Royal Dublin Society as an assistant to the Superintendent. I had literally just arrived in Ireland off the ferry at Dun Laoghaire with friends, on their horsebox for the Dublin Horse Show, and was looking for somebody who could organise a hotel room for me and a taxi to get me there. The person I asked sent me to 'the big boss'. That was Dermot. In the twenty minutes that we spent in his office, he managed to lose his pen seven times — a trait he never lost: with keys, pens, notepads, pagers, mobile phones. When I returned to the office to thank him, he offered to show me Dublin — things developed and I'm still here.

Those were the days of the Tinvane Hotel in Carrick-on-Suir where Robbie O'Connell lived. My first trip there and thus my first time seeing Dermot on stage were within three weeks of arriving in Ireland in August 1977. Those nights were magic, especially for a foreigner with romantic notions about Ireland like myself. The nights always finished very early in the morning with brilliant sessions. Our son Don's first long drive — he must have been all of six to eight weeks — was down to Tinvane. I remember keeping bottles with milk in the top of the pram where he slept, so that I could go straight to sleep again...

The gigs in Dublin that I remember were, amongst others, in the Suffolk House — a Wednesday evening session organised by Maura (I can't think of her surname but I'm sure she'll accept that it's not malice — just old age); the 'fee' was £3. That was £1 for just over a gallon of petrol and £2 for two pints each — yes, you did get change of a pound from two pints in those days. There were a number of occasional gigs, but the Suffolk House one was quite regular. The act was shaped and formed and the dog-collar appeared occasionally, but also the guitar and the parodies like '46B', about a well-known Dublin bus route, to the tune of 'Sloop John B'. Later the clothes were refined — I'm sure Sally Hogarty remembers the first 'tear-away' shirt (for quick character changes) and priest silks. I also remember the first 'international' gig in March 1978 in my hometown, Hamburg, in a little bar where Dermot sang (mainly ballads!). Even though there was no fee involved, mysteriously our drinks bill was paid by the end of the night.

Don was born in the 'strong winter of 1978' at a time when Dermot had changed from the RDS to the 'Wilson Scheme', a retraining of secondary teachers for use in primary schools. Nothing Dermot ever did was boring, so even a course like that had its other uses, in this case playing table tennis and other such delights. Late in 1978, the show in the Oscar Theatre with Alan Amsby proved to be something Dermot particularly enjoyed — never boring, never the same routine twice.

Don was born in the comfort of St Michael's nursing home in Dun Laoghaire and Dermot was caught there twice with brown paper bags — the first time with a bottle of champagne bought, I think, in 'Walter's Men's Bar'. The second occasion was a bit messier with a Chinese take-away seeping through...

There were few gigs in those days that I didn't go to, so some are quite vivid in my mind. Like the Widows' Association 'do' at which he told a joke that just 'came into his head' and turned out to be the noose around his neck. The joke was about a husband who comes home drunk and is met by an irate wife who asks him where he's been. 'At the graveyard,' he replies. 'Who's dead?' asks the wife, to her husband's reply 'All of them'. It did not go down well: the Gresham Hotel was never that silent again.

After the teaching course finished, Dermot started to teach in St Michael's. For anybody else that could have been the turning point to a 'settled life', but not for him. He enjoyed the letters to Mike Murphy for his radio show and the TV appearances on *The Live Mike*.

Around the time that he left St Michael's, Bobby was born: this poor kid was treated by his father to the view of the underside of a champagne-bottle. Bobby had decided to arrive on a bank holiday, leaving staff a little stretched in Loughlinstown Hospital, so they asked could they put him in an incubator while tidying up (mother still on drip) and the only place Dermot found for the champagne (this time bought in the Silver Tassie in a white plastic bag with ice) was on top of the incubator. Dermot was then better known as Father Trendy, resulting in a photo in an evening paper of us all in the hospital with Dermot dressed as Father Trendy and a headline saying 'Oh, Father'.

Dermot loved being a dad, even when the boys were very small and, as he often said, 'could sense a hangover like nothing else...' He was forever singing and playing with them and minding Bobby who was an extremely colicky baby. He could play rough and tumble with them (especially just before they were supposed to go to bed!) but also be very, very calm and show a crying child the moon in the middle of the night.

Something he always talked about when they were small, which he thankfully fulfilled with all three boys, was the ambition to bring them to football matches and 'lift them over the turnstiles'. When Don and Bobby were a little bit bigger and started to play football, he went with them as often as possible when they tried out for a number of clubs. I remember him telling a particular coach who had left one of them on the sideline during the whole match that the children were 'not playing European Championships but Sunday morning football'.

Dermot could get quite annoyed — I remember the theft of the 'green Goddess', his beloved light-green-metallic Cortina. We were at home in the evening and heard an engine revving up outside. By the time we got out she was turning round the corner. He was very upset and willing to act out everything the Kray twins could only dream of. We got her back, from the 'Ranch' in Ballyfermot, stripped of all the chrome she ever had, caked in mud and missing all the tapes. He brought her home and let the insurance company take over and take her away. That dream had ended.

Dermot loved reading and when he had a book he liked, he preferred to be left alone with it — which could be for a number of days on occasions. I remember the relief when he finished the book about Jimmy Boyle (a Glasgow heavy) and we often laughed about me threatening divorce at the time. In the late 1970s/early 1980s material like the Krays, Jimmy Boyle, et cetera fascinated him. He loved rhyming slang and TV programmes like *Minder*.

When Don, and later Bobby, started in kindergarten in the German School he got involved in organising soccer matches as part of their summerfest and to raise some funds for the school by involving the companies with which other parents were associated. That was the birth of the red 'Flamingos' team. 'Flamingos', for those who do not remember, was the disco in the erstwhile South County Hotel, near Mount Merrion. The red Flamingos played quite a lot for many good causes and I remember washing the jerseys regularly. They changed their plumage to pink with the big match for which Denis Waterman brought over his team. Those pink Flamingos played on for quite a long time. Soccer had always played a big part in Dermot's life, watching and playing as well as 'coaching', i.e. bringing a bunch of Don's and Bobby's pals down to Belfield to kick a ball around when they were still in kindergarten or primary school.

The few bits of snow we had on occasions always proved to be great fun with Dermot when he brought the boys 'up the mountains'. But my main memory is the big snow of January 1982, which coincided with the filming of *The Live Mike*. On the way back from the RTÉ studio the car got stuck in a snow drift outside the pub and we just left it there to catch a last pint. To Dermot's annoyance the barman was convinced it was five past eleven rather than five to eleven, but he got his pint in the end. We got the car going again only to get stuck in another snow drift outside the house. The hangover from copious hot whiskeys quickly vanished when he played with the boys in the snow the next day. Bobby was only eighteen months old at the time and the snow reached his waist! The following week Dermot portrayed the 'Minister for Snow' on *The Live Mike*, complete with a very long green scarf I had made years earlier in the days of maxi coats. Nowadays Don wears scarves from those days — it's nice to see the next generation being interested in the same things as the previous one.

Dermot often found things that interested him as well as the boys, be it football, cinema, TV or whatever. In their younger years they enjoyed trips to the beach, fishing or to the 'Hairy Monster' (the car wash) when they were quite small. On one of the first fishing trips — they must have been around eight or nine years of age — Bobby caught a little flounder, smaller than the palm of his hand. There was a certain amount of joint pride and upset about the little fish. We ate the other ones the three of them had caught on that trip. They never got that conger eel though. Their fishing trips were repeated in later years and as they grew so did the fish.

Earlier on, Dermot didn't want to leave Mount Merrion; later after we had grown apart, myself, Don and Bobby stayed there. He was never quite at ease visiting us there but I'm glad his sons have had the chance to live in the house in which he grew up in and hopefully in years to come their children will be the fourth generation of Morgans to still be at that house.

There are no training courses to prepare you for parenthood, but Dermot did not need one. He acted on instinct and impulse and was a good, a very, very good father, even at the beginning. Thankfully we always remained friends and he continued to be a good father to the boys. In fact, I couldn't have wished for a better one for them.

THANK YOU VERY MUCH...

Bobby and I were only growing up in the 1980s but we still remember some of the things that were going on in that decade and that mark those years as a time in our lives.

One of the things was that Dermot began to play a lot of football again. He'd played at school and in college, but in our lifetimes the football began in the early Eighties. It was around then that he and some friends started the Flamingos football team, sponsored by Flamingos night-club. They chiefly took part in fund-raisers for charities and for the school Bobby and I were attending — St Kilian's German School, in Clonskeagh — where Dermot played a role in organising the fund raising from time to time. I can just about remember a huge yellow beer tent that they put up for the post-match celebrations.

One of the highlights of the Flamingos experience was in 1983 when they played against a celebrity XI, captained by Denis Waterman, of *Minder* fame. It was a big enough 'do' and took place in the Old Belvedere rugby club in Ballsbridge in aid of Rehab. It was great fun, watching Dermot and his friends making fools of themselves on the pitch. Actually they weren't that bad, and it was all done for the fun of the thing. In fact, their greatest success on that occasion was not on the pitch at all, but at Dublin airport when they went to meet Denis and his team. Dermot and Pat Finn came across a motorcycle Garda and managed to persuade him — I don't know how — to give the visiting team an escort back into the city, with flashing lights and siren blaring. Denis and his friends were suitably impressed — but Dermot and Pat were even more impressed with themselves at the feat they had managed to pull off!

Dermot's career also seemed to be picking up in those years. There certainly were moments when things looked like they might work; that he would get the break that he craved for. In 1983, it looked as if he would get his own television show on RTÉ, imaginatively titled *The Dermot Morgan Show*. It was going to be a show filled with sketches and things like that; a vehicle for Dermot's talents. As far as I remember, there was a lot of input into the project from people such as the producer of the show, John Keogh, and Dermot's friends, Barry Devlin and Michael Redmond, who contributed to the writing and in general by bandying ideas around. However, I don't think they formally collaborated as such: it was only later on that Dermot and Barry began to collaborate formally on writing. They both found that, at that stage, they would be entirely incompatible working together. (No doubt, they would have just fought a lot.)

The show was filmed and the series took shape during late 1982 and 1983 with a reasonable amount of success. They managed to get together six to nine episodes, constructed in a sketch-type format. But apart from those he had around him — John Keogh, Barry and Michael — Dermot didn't have a writing partner or even a team of writers who could help him to bring a structure to the show, say in the way someone like John Cleese did with Graham Chapman in Monty Python. RTÉ left him more or less to his own devices, throwing some money at him and letting him get on with making the show for them. This, I should point out, is my opinion from what I have gathered from people I've spoken to. There is a feeling amongst some of those that Dermot worked with on the show that he was very much left hanging in the wind, writing by himself without getting the support he would have got in England or in America. That said, the show was taking shape well.

The fact it was looking good, albeit raw, makes it very strange that RTÉ then shelved it rather suddenly. Before anyone knew what was going on, RTÉ had handed the tapes over to editors who condensed the series into a one-hour special. I remember it nearly killed him. He was extremely glum and very down about everything, and had little if any confidence anymore in what he did. I never knew, until someone told me around the time of his funeral, that he had had to retrieve the tapes of the series out of a bin in RTÉ's archives himself. That must have been the final humiliation in that whole episode.

The one-hour *Dermot Morgan Special*, was broadcast in June 1983. It got some good reviews but for Dermot its success was tarnished by what had happened to the series it should have been. Some journalists asked why RTÉ didn't have more of that kind of thing on the air. It seemed that they just never had and never could deal with that kind of comedy.

For a while afterwards, Dermot didn't really do much of anything in the way of work. Anyone would feel the way he felt if something for which they had worked and craved and finally seen becoming tangible disappeared so suddenly. And he'd also had his source of income cut off. He never forgot what had happened to *The Dermot Morgan Show* and it probably made him a lot wiser about life and about how things worked in this country. As with every disappointment he suffered though, it also made him more determined to get his point across, and he kept going.

It took him months after that to pick up the pieces of his career. But he kept his mind going during that time by writing; he was always scribbling something down. I have this image of him sitting in the kitchen at breakfast, hunched over his cumbersome blue electric typewriter, staring at it, his mouth chewing invisible gum, before pouncing on the machine, bashing the keys as he came up with new ideas. He wrote almost compulsively, putting down whatever ideas came into his head. Over that time, he continued to knock around concepts with his friends, and with people who also wrote — basically, like in college, with anyone who had the same sense of badness as he. Those sessions could take place anywhere and in any situation, if the mood was right.

During the times he didn't have much actual work, he still found things to do. He played a hell of a lot of football, and watched a lot of it too. That's when I remember him starting to take Bobby and me to football matches. He'd take us to see UCD's team play in their home venue, a tiny 'stadium' in a corner of the college campus in Belfield. This was always a lot of fun and something that we still do to this day.

After the game against Denis Waterman's team, the Flamingos played here and there, but I don't think they really played all that much from the mid-1980s. They never quite stopped, continuing as if in 'semi-retirement'. The last game I remember them playing was when Shamrock Rovers, one of Dublin's most established football clubs, had sold their home ground, Glenmalure Park in Milltown. Dermot organised a match in protest between Flamingos, which featured Def Leppard's Joe Elliot who was as football-mad as Dermot, and a team led by Dublin restaurateur Patrick Guillbaud. Dermot was very upset that the stadium, which was part of Dublin, had been sold off to make way for a housing estate.

Apart from that, footie after the mid-1980s was mostly played in five-a-sides made up of more or less the same crowd that had been playing in Flamingos. They ended up playing twice a week, in St Kilian's German school in Clonskeagh and in St Andrew's in Booterstown. It was, and still is, great fun and Dermot was in the thick of it, playing with huge amounts of enthusiasm, even if he wasn't the greatest player of all time. But they had fun and that's all that matters really. They still play regularly and Bobby and I join them occasionally.

The early 1980s always seemed to me to be sporadic in relation to work. Dermot gigged a lot and he told me years later that the following year — 1984 — was a good year for him. He regained his confidence, picked up the pieces and began all over again. He did a lot of different things to make a living in those years — gigs, the occasional voice-over for ads, openings for this and that — and just kept plugging away with scripts and more scripts, a lot of which still hold their own when looked at now. They might be a little dated as a lot of the stuff was topical but much of it is good and some of it gives a hint as to the kind of topical satire that would become famous later with *Scrap Saturday*.

He also did a potentially brilliant project for a show called *Good Morning, Europe* which was a piss-take of the new satellite stations at the time. It was going to be presented by another character he had created, Eddie Van Dringen, a send-up of the Dutch television presenters that used to pop up on Sky Television when it first started out, complete with some of the worst mullet hair-dos[*] on earth. Wonderful. I can still remember the amount of work he put into that project — video promos, dry runs, and scripts of

---

[*] For those not familiar with the 'mullet', it may help to think about the classic footballers' hairstyle of the early 1980s: short at the sides and on top, but long and flowing at the back.

what the show would be like. It was a very professional job but, for some reason or another, it never got anywhere. I've always wondered why.

Many of his subsequent characters took shape in those years of the early 1980s in informal collaborations and conspiracies with his friends. His closest friends were known as The Committee, the people with whom he conspired, watched football and went out. The core group was Dermot himself, Donagh Morgan, Pat Finn and Peter Redmond, although there were several others involved as well.

One thing that took a particular hold of his imagination at that period, although he kept it low-key in his work until later, was the idea for the character known as Jim, the rugger fanatic. Jim was one of the products of sessions with Pat Finn and the Redmond brothers, Peter and Michael, and was a source of in-jokes among them for years, usually in the pub or in gatherings of that nature. (All the characters he did in public shows were a lot tamer than the private versions of them he did among his friends!) Both Peter and Michael were particularly observant of certain mannerisms and Dermot and his friends allowed this Jim monster to take on a life of his own. It was only later that he thought of using Jim in any of his shows, culminating in a monologue he did for the Amnesty International *So You Think You're Funny* festival in the Gaiety Theatre in Dublin a few years ago.

Dermot even appeared in a film at one stage in the 1980s. It was a small part in an Irish film called *Taffin*, which starred Pierce Brosnan, when most people knew him as Remington Steel, as opposed to James Bond. Dermot played a stand-up comedian of all things while Frank Kelly, who later became the famous Father Jack in *Father Ted*, played a cheery Irish barman! Dermot's character was called Mickey

Guest, a total scumbag complete with a glitzy suit. The filming was done in Wicklow and, from what I remember, Dermot only really had a few days at most on the set. But we had a lovely trip down to Wicklow Town for an afternoon whilst Dermot was up on the set.

For a time he was also a columnist for the *Sunday Tribune* and later on for the *Evening Herald*. For the shortest of times he even had a small slot called *Printweek* on an afternoon television show on RTÉ in which he reviewed the week's newspapers. Those were all things which kept him going but they weren't really what he wanted to do, although the experience was probably useful to him.

One of the most successful things he did in that period was to make records. In the early 1980s he had a song called *The Taoiseach's Lament*, which was a parody of a Harp Lager ad that was out at the time and took off the then Taoiseach, Charles Haughey. I don't know if it did well, but apparently it was pretty good. Then in 1985, he had a big hit with *Thank You Very Much Mr. Eastwood*. This was written about former world featherweight boxing champion Barry McGuigan's incessant thanking of his manager at the time, Barney Eastwood. In fact it was the Christmas Number One in Ireland and Dermot got a gold disc for his efforts.

My memories of Christmas mornings at the time are still vivid because we always had parties, with the grown-ups getting pissed, and all of us having a whale of a time. That particular Christmas morning, he did a live radio interview from home with Larry Gogan or one of those DJs on RTÉ's 2FM. There was the usual big party going on in the house but there was a whole extra sense of madness about it that year. As far as I can make out, the madness seeped onto the airwaves, providing a lot of background noise to his interview.

Thank You Very Much Mr. Eastwood got into the British charts as well and it received a lot of play, for some reason, on TV AM. They even made a video for it, which Dermot got a great kick out of doing. It allowed him to dress up as a whole lot of different people, not just as Barry McGuigan, but also as the Pope, Bob Geldof, and a brilliant Ronald Reagan. He had a ball.

There was one irony to the song, though. Barry Devlin had produced the single. As some will remember, Barry was the bassist with *Horslips*, a big Celtic rock outfit in the early 1970s, but they had never had a Number One. They once got to Number Two, but that was it. So this was Barry's first Number One. Funny that...

In 1986 Dermot got a TV series on RTÉ in the shape of a game show called *Jackpot*. It had been done originally in the 1960s when it was presented by the likes of Gay Byrne and a young Terry Wogan. So now Dermot had the honour. One of those involved in it was none other than Declan Lowney, who eventually directed a series of *Father Ted*. Dermot presented the show for one season: apparently there were some people who thought that he was taking the piss out of it and of game shows generally — he certainly had a very cheesy look about him when he was doing it! However, it was successful and it did him some good, mainly because it gave him some more experience. It was the first regular substantial television work he got, but it still wasn't exactly what he wanted in the way of his own show.

It was followed some time later by more regular television work when Pat Kenny, a friend and colleague of Dermot's over the years, was starting a new talk-show called *Kenny Live*. Kenny had worked with Dermot years previously and knew his capabilities, so he invited Dermot to provide the more satirical elements of the show. As he recalls it:

> We were asked in 1988 to design *Kenny Live* as an alternative to the *Late Late Show*. It seemed obvious that Dermot, who was no longer working in *The Live Mike* which had been finished a couple of years at that stage, was available and it seemed like a scandalous waste of his talent that he wasn't being given work and we just jumped at the chance.

As far as I can remember, Dermot enjoyed the experience. He was doing something which was as close as possible to what he wanted to do and he was having fun doing it. A lot of stuff he did on the show, not unlike what he had done previously on *The Live Mike*, was the toughest (as well as the only) satire on Irish television. They had a few close shaves with libel as well as ruffling a few feathers. Dermot did a couple of seasons on the show until it was restructured to a more strictly talk-show format.

Towards the end of the 1980s, he had three other singles, *Do You Know Bono?*, *Get Out of That Saddle, Stephen*, (about Stephen Roche's victory in the Tour de France) and *Daddy's in Deutschland* (which was for the Irish team in Germany for the European Cup). The first two reached the top five of the charts in Ireland and *Daddy's in Deutschland* also sold well.

In 1987, he released an album called *Special Moments*, which is complete with a cheesy cover of Dermot looking slick in a tuxedo, holding a bottle of champagne and a bag of greasy chips. It was basically a collection of the songs he had already released as singles at the time alongside some new material. He took Bobby and me around to Stark Studios in the centre of Dublin to see him record it. It was intriguing for a nine-year old, seeing all the strange stuff they had there. What I remember most is the way Dermot showed us all around it — not just around the obvious parts but all the backrooms as well — and demonstrated the way things worked, like how you attached all the microphones to stands. I suppose I got more detail than a nine-year-old really wanted to know.

So the 1980s had some good things going on for him. At a time when there was only sporadic television work available to him and stand-up was still in its infancy in Ireland, he liked singing songs, from folk to parody songs, which also made him a few shillings. Of the tons of songs he'd composed many were written out of amusement but some came out of the anger which often fuelled what he did.

For example, he hated the Provisional IRA. He couldn't understand or accept that element of Irish life and the sort of ballads that went with it. I guess, in general, he hated bigotry of any description but that particular type really, really disturbed him. So he wrote a few songs satirising the musicians who sang rebel songs, like the folk band The Wolfe Tones.

There were two songs in particular which showed his dislike of Brit-bashing and that whole genre — *Alsatian Once Again*, which ended with a parody of the chorus to *A Nation Once Again* and was about a dog who was blown up for Irish freedom, and the brutally funny *Robert Emmet's Head*, about the execution of Robert Emmet in 1803 which ended with a slow verse rant in the style of a traditional lament about the British killing Hitler.

The final singles he did were in the 1990s, when his production company, Cue Productions, was already up and running. One was for the World Cup in 1990, *Mama Mia, What A Beautiful Team*. The other was around the time *Scrap Saturday* ended, when Albert Reynolds, known for being a dance hall owner, became Taoiseach — called *A Country and Western Taoiseach*. They also sold pretty well.

From our point of view, the 1980s were kind of fun as Bobby and I were growing up and doing a lot of things with Dermot. We played football with him in the front garden, which was destroyed, much to our mother's dismay; as our German grandfather used to comment, 'one shot, one flower'. Most of the time it would be him against us; sometimes Dermot would drag Bobby and myself out of bed so he and Pat Finn could play us. We usually beat them. Actually, I took the legs off Dermot one time and he was limping for a week. For some reason though he was more amused — 'my son crippled me!' — than upset that I'd done that, at least as time went by.

In general, though, the 1980s were a giant learning curve for Dermot. He had developed as a writer to the point where he wasn't as naïve as when he was a student. He had more experience as a stand-up and that scene was changing for the better. He had more experience, too, of television. He had seen the lows of the world he worked in and now knew how to play hardball when necessary. Sooner or later, things would come together for him.

Songs, Skits

and Other Bits

What follows are the lyrics of some of Dermot's most successful songs from the 1980s, staring off with the Number One hit, *Thank You Very Much, Mr Eastwood*, and including his satirical versions of standard rebel ballads: *Robert Emmet's Head* and *Alsatian Once Again*. They are followed by some skits and sketches mostly from Dermot's 98FM radio show, *Guten Morgan*, and some of Dermot's articles from *The Sunday Tribune*. All in all, a flavour of what he was doing in the 1980s…

Thank You Very Much, Mr. Eastwood

Barry McGuigan::

I was standing there in the ring in the Kings Hall, so I
    was,
I was still the World Champion after it all.
Well the fans were all leaving and the lights they grew
    dim,
I'd finished the fighting and started the thanking.

So I'm saying Thank You, Thank You, Thank You very,
    very, very much Mr. Eastwood.
Thanks mum and dad and my brothers and sister,
But the man I thank most is the man I call Mister.
Mr. Eastwood.

Thank You, Thank You, Thank You very, very, very
    much Mr. Eastwood.

Backing Singers:

Thank You, Thank You, Thank You very, very, very
    much, Mr. Eastwood.
Thanks for the telegrams everyone sent,
like the one from the States and their President.

President Regan:

Well I don't know much about, I don't know much
    Harry, but I guess Scotland are proud of you

Barry McGuigan:

Mr. President you should thank Mr. Eastwood!

President Regan:

Okay, so I say, Thank You, Thank You, Thank You very,
    very, very much Mr.... Err..."
Thanks to his mom and poppa, his brother and his
    sister.
But the one he thanks most is the one he calls err...

Backing Singers:

 Thank you very, very, very much Mr. Eastwood.
Thank you very, very, very much Mr. Eastwood.

Barry McGuigan:

You've a cut said me trainer you need a Band-Aid.
So Bob Geldof arrived and I knew I was made, so I did.

Bob Geldof:

Like Barry you're amazing, like. You deserve all the
    credit for being so amazingly bloody good.

Barry McGuigan:
I said Bob, all the credit to Mr. Eastwood.

Bob Geldof:
OK, so we're saying thank you, like, thank you, right,
   thank you very, very, very much Mr. Eastwood.
   He's thanking his mum and his dad, his brother
   and his sister. But the man he thanks most is the
   man he calls Mister.

Bob and Backing singers:
Thank you very, very, very much Mr. Eastwood.

Barry McGuigan:
So I took off me gloves and I leaned on the rope,
   thanking the audience.
   And I pick up the phone, who was there but the
   Pope.

Pope John Paul:
Young Barry, I love you and I thank God that you are
   so good.

Barry McGuigan:
Don't thank him Your Holiness, thank Mr. Eastwood.

Pope and Backing Singers:
So we say thank you, thank you, thank you very, very
   very much Mr. Eastwood.
Thanks mum and dad and his brother and his sister.
But the man he thanks most is the one he calls Mister

Barry McGuigan::

Thanks to Sandra, and to Blaine they're a bonus, and
thanks to the fans here and the ones back in
Clones.
Thanks to me trainer, me doctor, me solicitor.
But the man I thank most is the one I call... Mister.

Robert Emmet's Head

Last night I had a dream and it nearly made me
    scream,
I dreamt I walked the streets of Dublin town.
And down by Thomas Street something rolled and hit
    my feet,
It had eyes and hair, a nose and it was round.

And it was Robert Emmet's head,
The English killed him dead, it's been rolling round the
    streets since God knows when.
But it's easy now to see, he's lost the personality,
And nothing like us United Irish men.

Boys and Girls...

In 1803 people in Dublin turned to see what blew up
    and made the noise that bounced down Camden
    Street,
When the traffic lights turned red what pulled up but
    Emmet's head,
A better head you couldn't hope to meet,

And it was Robert Emmet's head,
The English killed him dead, it's been rolling round the
    streets since God knows when.
Now the Brit's they were the pits when poor old
    Emmet went to bits
A United Irishman he'll never be.

He was hung and drawn and quartered and the rising
    was aborted,
extremely dead our patriotic giant.

But even though he's dead, the only better head you'll
    ever come across is on a pint.

And it was Robert Emmet's head,
The English killed him dead, it's been rolling round the
    streets since God knows when.
But it's easy now to see, he's lost the personality,
and nothing like us United Irish men.

(slow verse)

Ah, they murdered poor Hitler with their cruel hearted
    bombing,
They called him a Nazi, no Nazi was he.
But they made such a fuss of his little Anschluss which
    was only designed to set Austria free.

Bastards.

Mama Mia

In an art gallery in Florence the experts gathered
    round,
to view an undiscovered masterpiece just lately found.
When the curtains fell they mumbled "It's painted all
    in Green!"
It wasn't the Last Supper, but Jackie Charlton's team.

Mama Mia, Mama Mia, what a beautiful team,
the one Jack built the, one in emerald green.
They're singing it in St Peter's and the Coliseum.
Mama Mia, Mama Mia, what a beautiful team.

In Roma I met Bono,
who was standing there on Edge.
("Get off me Bono")
Who wasn't very happy, but Bono said I pledge
"I'm sorry I must leave you, it's not that I've found God,
it's just that I've been offered a place in Jackie
    Charlton's squad."

Mama Mia, Mama Mia, what a beautiful team,
the one Jack built the, one in emerald green.
They're singing it in St Peter's and the Coliseum.
Mama Mia, Mama Mia, what a beautiful team.

Outside La Scala I met Pavarotti,
he was snotty, I asked "What's wrong?"
he said "Although I like to sing Aida, I feel that I needa,
to sing a new song."
Like...
Mama Mia, Mama Mia, what a beautiful team,
the one Jack built the, one in emerald green.
They're singing it in St Peter's and the Coliseum.

Mama Mia, Mama Mia, what a beautiful team.

Outside of the Vatican I stopped and asked of the
    Swiss Guard,
"what's the greatest sight in Rome?"
The soldier he thought real hard.
"We have galleries, the seven hills and even a
    museum."
A voice upstairs said,
"Tell the truth, it's Jackie Charlton's team."

Mama Mia, Mama Mia, what a beautiful team,
the one Jack built the, one in emerald green.
They're singing it in St Peter's and the Coliseum.
Mama Mia, Mama Mia, what a beautiful team.

In the Trevi Fountain there will be every sort to meet,
Dubs swimming and some Culchies just down to
    wash their feet.
Milan is full of Mayo men,
Roscommon's gone to Rome.
Men from Ennis are in Venice feeling quite at home.

Mama Mia, Mama Mia, what a beautiful fans,
Not lager louts but the ones who sing and dance.
They've got to be the greatest fans the world has ever
    seen.
Mama Mia, Mama Mia, and a beautiful team.

I dreamt I got to heaven,
there was many a famous face.
Except for Eamonn Dunphy who was in the "other"
    place.
When I saw St Peter I really had to laugh,
he was queuing up with pen in hand, for Jackie's
    autograph.

Mama Mia, Mama Mia, what a beautiful team,
the one Jack built the, one in emerald green.
They're singing it in St Peter's and the Coliseum.
Mama Mia, Mama Mia, what a beautiful team.

Mama Mia, Mama Mia, what a beautiful team,
the one Jack built the, one in emerald green.
They're singing it in St Peter's and the Coliseum.
Mama Mia, Mama Mia, what a beautiful team.

Alsatian Once Again

(Spoken Introduction)

Many songs are sung about Emmett, Pearse and Tone.
But no one knows that son of Ireland who loved to
    chew a bone.
A Patriot so fearless who fought doggedly for his
    nation.
Not a Catholic or Protestant, but a bloody big Alsatian.

Way back in 1920 when the troubles were real bad.
The Black and Tans were searching houses, driving
    people mad.
Many Irish men and Women lent a hand to help the
    cause.
Here is a story of hero who lent a pair of paws.

(Chorus)

And it was Fido, hid the hand grenade for me,
when the Tans came round to search the house at
    tea.
I said "Fido, take this, eat!"
He thought it was a tin of meat.
It was the hand grenade that Fido hid for me.

*

The Black and Tans they searched the house but not a
    thing they found.
They checked for guns and bullets,
but they never checked the hound.
They scorned and marched and jeered us,

but their laughter ended soon.
When Fido just exploded and splattered around the
room.

(Chorus)

And it was Fido hid the hand grenade for me,
when the Tans came round to search the house at
tea.
The Tans said " Excuse me mate, was that something
your dog ate?"
It was the hand grenade that Fido hid for me.

*

The Tans run out in terror,
Fido saved us one and all.
So I looked there and he lay there on the ceiling, wall
and floor.
Another martyr for old Ireland by Britannia cruelly
slain.
Some day up there I hope he'll be an Alsatian once
again.

(To the tune of 'A Nation Once again')

Alsatian once again,
Alsatian once again.
And Fido now in heaven will be
an Alsatian once again!

Queen of the Checkouts

(Sung in a style reminiscent of Johnny Cash)

I was looking at my loved one as I walked down the
    aisle,
But she just kept her head down she never saw my
    smile.
It was Friday it was my pay day, I grabbed half a
    dozen stout,
I loaded them and wheeled my trolley straight to her
    checkout.

No I'll not forget how she grabbed the mike, saying
    "Manager to the checkout please. And sign the
    gentleman's cheque and take his fishfingers off my
    knees."
As she rattled my Rice Krispies,
she threw my spuds about.
But I made a special offer to the Queen of the
    Checkouts.

So it's Friday, I go shopping just so I could look at her,
and I just stand and watch her hand as it touched the
    cash register.
I was hiding among some pet foods,
just between some Pal and Chum.
When I got hit twice with a 99p price from a great fire
    labelling gun.

She put the Super in Supermarket and she was sweet
    to me,
she even laughed and said I put a Gross in Grocery.
As she clung to my cling foil and weighed my brussel
    sprouts,

No wonder I went off my trolley for the Queen of the
    checkouts.

Oh, I staggered to her checkout, I felt, I felt at ease.
Just because my face is 99p it don't mean, it don't
    mean that I'm cheap.
She just loaded me in her trolley, whose front wheels
    were both turned out.
And I swerved and wobbled home with her, the
    Queen of the Checkouts.

Oh, how she totted up the items and she could hit
    those keys,
smiling she would turn and say "Hey, Rita. How much
    are these?"
Amid the sounds of music, the roars and all the
    shouts,
I gave my heart and some Kellogg's Start to the
    Queen of the Checkouts.

She put the Super in Supermarket,
and she was sweet to me.
She even laughed and said I put the Gross in Grocery.
As she clung to my cling foil and weighed my brussel
    sprouts,
No wonder I went off my trolley for the Queen of the
    Checkouts.

Don't Pick Wardie

This song is about the mysterious reluctance of the Irish Rugby Football Union to pick Tony Ward for the Irish team in the 1980s when he was widely regarded as one of the best players around. Dermot's 'Jim the Rugger-Bugger' character sang this one.

You can pick Joe with a broken toe,
but don't pick Wardie.
You can pick Dean or any human being,
But don't pick Wardie.

Wardie always went too far,
he became a superstar.
Players needn't all be mugs,
but he appeared in his swimming trunks.

You can pick Keyes, be my guest please,
but don't pick Wardie.
My word, bye golly you can pick Ollie,
but you know what I mean.

He's not my choice Mister,
he's not even a bloody solicitor.
You can pick Mother or AN Other,
but leave Wardie off the team.

You can go for our Hugo,
but don't pick Wardie.
Brilliant Keith, marvellous feet,
but don't pick Wardie.

Sure the Welsh all work in mines,
shouldn't our lads work for mine.

And he'll never get my vote,
he doesn't even wear a sheepskin coat.

You can pick Keyes be my guest please,
but don't pick Wardie.
You can pick Trevor doesn't matter, whoever,
but Wardie's not my style.

Now you know I'm no knocker,
it's just he used to play soccer.
It makes me sick he's far to slick,
Lets bring back Jack Kyle.

You can pick Joe with a broken toe,
but don't pick Wardie.
You can pick Dean or any human being,
But don't pick Wardie.

We don't mind Mick Kiernan on,
we know his dad and his uncle Tom.
But it makes me histrionic,
Wardie doesn't even drink Gin & Tonic.

You can pick Thatcher if you can catch her,
but don't pick Wardie.
You can pick Bridget or a one-legged midget,
but keep Wardie off the team.

My wife said it shocked her,
to hear he's not even a doctor.
He's too swarthy, that chap Wardie,
makes me sick, he's far too slick.
You can pick Mother or AN Other
Keep Wardie off the team.

The Football Commentator

Interviewer: Eamonn, what did you think of it as a
                contest?

Eamonn Dunphy:

Well in the long run, at the end of the day
the result hinged largely on the abilities of
the Allies to get men forward in strength but
in fairness to the Germans they had very
well-organised defence, played with a lot of
skill but I think they lost the head towards
the end... against that you have to look at
the lad Patton and the lad Bradley while
beyond any doubt Churchill is an old-
fashioned English dribbler and as for the
way he kept giving two fingers I'm surprised
he wasn't sent off... at end of the day I think
it was the right result... though I was
appalled at some of the boy Hitler's actions...
he went in hard on everyone but my biggest
regret was that if he did have to persecute a
minority why not the FAI Executive
Committee... I do it myself.

The Israelis Arrive

I found this script in a box in a file called Guten Morgan, *dated May 25th 1985. It was a collaboration with Paddy Murray and various other people. This is a mock news report of the late president of Israel, the Irish-born Chaim Herzog, visiting Ireland and his dramatic stay at the Berkeley Court Hotel in Ballsbridge, Dublin.*

REPORTER:

Chaim Herzog's visit to Ireland has been a graphic demonstration of Israeli policy. The government agreed that when Mr. Herzog came here he would be entitled to a hotel suite like anyone else coming to these shores. Mr. Herzog duly took up residence in the hotel suite allocated to him but insisted that in the interests of his own security he must rid adjacent suites of potentially threatening residents.

Accordingly the Israeli party have swept through the entire floor of the hotel insisting that they will withdraw to their own quarters once the floor is secure.

The hotel management has given assurances that the other guests are not hostile but the offer of the hotel's management is being scorned by the Israeli party who say the hotel management is weak and ineffectual.

It was yesterday morning that room service in the form of a fanatical waitress arrived in the Israeli suite and threw breakfast at the sleepy president announcing in the local dialect: "There's yer shaggin' breakfast."

Israeli reaction was swift and ruthless. They ran through the hotel spraying scrambled egg and spilling hot coffee over all the guests.

At present Herzog will not withdraw to his room only, and he and his men now occupy all his floor, the floor below him and the floor above him and his men are now building a settlement in the penthouse floor to give them a commanding view of the surrounding accommodation.

While they have now secured the Berkeley Court, it came as a complete surprise when the Israeli officials launched a lightning raid on nearby Jury's to clear the bar which they said represented a clear threat of singing and rowdiness.

The night porters and reception desks have been captured and coats in the cloakroom have been rounded up. The Israelis are still mopping up operations in the kitchen. The Israelis want the entire hotel and are prepared to fight to rid it of other guests. The Americans have offered to pay the bill but there is still no sign of the Israelis calling a taxi. This is an extremely serious reporter with one of those tense and breathless deliveries handing back to the studio.

The Golf Commentator

Although Dermot tried over the years to come to terms with golf, he never quite grasped it. Birdies and bogeys and whatever they have in that game, which make it more difficult to understand than most things in this world. I suppose that's why he loved football.

SPORTS REPORTER: Well what a fascinating contest this year's contest is turning out to be with Trevino trailing Langer and Ballesteros bogeying on five of the back nine having eagled on the seventh and recorded no less than eight birdies on the way out, opting for a one iron in preference to a wood from the tee on the twelfth, having putted on the fifteenth to leave Langer needing an Albatross on the last hole to trail him by one in the clubhouse...

ANNOUNCER: And a translation of that report will soon be available in book-shops...

Schizophrenia

New York Gentleman: I'll take the last of those bagels over there, Mrs. Gurvits. Hey, by the way, have I told you about my son?

Mrs. Gurvits: No, Mr. Schlumberd, tell me about the ungrateful schtick. What's he done now?

NY Gentleman: He's a Schizophrenic.

Mrs. Gurvits: Really? A Schizophrenic? Where's his office?

Bus Queue

(Hubbub of voices protesting, a few female cries and over it conductor shouting...)

Conductor: Back! Get back the whole lot of youse. There's no boardin' this bus until ye're initiated into the etiquette and proper procedure for queuin'!

(Voices protest again....)

Conductor: None of your 'buffalo stamping' here, what we want is a bit of finesse... Now you madam with the broken umbrella... now ye must try to get on first with it *open...* yeah, that's it... hook the broken rib onto that young one's earring...

(Scream of pain)

Conductor: ... that's right, but you only got one person in the eye, go back and try again, you'll have to do better than that... close it now and prod the old lady in front of you with the steel tip...

(Another scream)

Conductor: ... very good... and you, Head... you with the outsize rucksack... you have to knock at least two people backwards wi' it as you hoist it on your shoulders...

(Yells of 'watch out,' 'oh me nose!' etc.)

Conductor:	...no, wait a minute, you didn't wedge your rucksack between the door and the bar, effectively blocking anyone from boarding on this side – I mean you might as well do the thing right or not at all...
Voice:	Thash me... the inevitable drunk!
Conductor:	Now Sir, I want you to throw your arm in a half-Nelson around that nun's neck and haul yourself on board... yes, very good... not bad, not bad... And finally, you Sir, what's the one question a passenger in a queue should never ask?
Man's voice:	Eh, what time does the bus leave?
Conductor:	Anyone who asks that question is told... what?
Chorus of passengers:	The one behind is pulling out first!!!
Conductor:	Eggactly! And as the person leaves and goes back to the bus behind, what do we do? We close the doors immediately, rev up the engine and pull away fast!
	(Murmur of voices again...)
Conductor:	Right! That was just a dry run, so to speak, heh!... heh!... heh!... – everybody off! *(Chorus of protesting voices...No! Why? Etc.)*
Conductor:	Because we're going to the garage, that's why! Are yeh right Mick?
	(Sound of bell...engine starting up and the bus pulling away.)

The GAA Fanatic

This was the hurley-wielding maniac who featured on The Live Mike *television show. This example, for instance, was at the end of a show as the host, Mike Murphy, wrapped it up and the credits began to roll. The GAA man wants to take issue with comments Mike Murphy made during the show about higher powers...*

GAA MAN: I want to protest – this is typical of RTÉ – you have made a mockery of everything we hold sacred here tonight – Laughed at Devine in most wicked blasphemy I have ever witnessed. It is a disgrace but no surprise coming from you shower up here. The Family League were right – you have attacked our whole set of values – with your Dallas and what have you – and put soccer on our screens – soccer – I ask you – in this Island we don't want that sort of dirty foreign culture and now tonight, you have sunk to the lowest – you have mocked at and jeered the Almighty himself – the most...

MIKE: Hold on there, I don't think God would be offended.

GAA MAN: I'm not talking about GOD – I'm talking about Charlie Haughey – how dare you! (HURLEY STICK BRANDISHED) Take that sneer off your face, Mick Murphy...

In the mid-1980s Dermot was a Sunday Tribune *columnist.
Following is a selection of articles published during this time.*

05/02/84

CIA Spills The Beans

ONCE AGAIN THE *TRIBUNE* gets a scoop. I have gone to some trouble to lay my hands on an extremely sensitive document. Wearing a helmet and visor, shoulder pads and a shirt with a large 22 emblazoned on the front, I strolled into the American Embassy armed only with an American football and a hamburger. Pausing only to genuflect before the large picture of John Wayne, I quickly made my way to an office and proceeded to rifle a filing cabinet marked "Top Secret". There I found the lot, the CIA briefing files on Ireland, suggested itinerary for the June visit — I even got a copy of President Reagan's speech.

The CIA report was interesting to say the least.

> "It is *essential*, repeat *essential* that the Presidential limousine does not travel from the airport through the thoroughfare known as Gardiner Street. We do not have the logistical backup to find new tyres for a Ford Lincoln at short notice. Equally it must be stressed that the First Lady does not, repeat does *not* keep her handbag on the seat beside her."

The report goes on:

> "This trip will have been made at too high a price if the President buys anything in the shops here. The Federal Budget has no provision for such an economic catastrophe."

On the President's public appearance, the CIA suggests that a US Airforce tanker be emptied, rinsed out and refuelled with hair colourant to supply the President with the volume of the liquid he requires.

They simply do not have those quantities of hair colouring in this country.

The report naturally has gone out of its way to identify dangerous groups: "To the best of our knowledge the Dubs do not present a threat to the President, unless he appears on the same field as them…" The CIA have also correctly identified CIE as the nation's organised crime. They are still checking out the "organised" aspect of it.

Seeking to clarify dissident groups, the CIA say "The group most feared by the government are known as brucellosis reactors. At the time of writing we do not have a positive ID on these, but when the government apprehends any they give them the "14-day test" which we imagine is some sort of third degree or a polymath at least."

"Intelligence on the ground and feedback from the local population leaves no doubt in our mind as to who is the most dangerous man in Ireland. He is universally feared and the mere mention of his name causes nervous reactions from people. He is known as Maurice Pratt."

On the positive side they concede that "Ireland is a country relatively free from prejudice, a national characteristic encouraged by the absence of blacks, wops, dagos, Polacks or gooks and boy do they know how to deal with faggots! The Agency respectfully suggests that Charles Bronson make his next movie on location in Fairview Park."

So much for the CIA, now a section from the President's speech.

"We in the United States are aware of the great friendship that exists and continues to grow between the people of our two nations. The increase in the number of hamburger and fried chicken parlours is proof of this and a warning to the Soviets. They are the proof of the contribution that we make to each others' rich and varied culture. In the mouths of Irish men and women is not only displayed their great heritage of literary work, that great love of language but also the Big Mac.

"We realise the love the Irish have for the people of America when we hear your great Country & Western ballad bands, bands like Big Tom and Larry Cunningham's, bands we hope the Irish will always keep in Ireland, bands which will be a warning to would-be Soviet invaders.

"Nancy and I want you to know that we love your rashers and eggs, your Guinness, your Baileys, your Bainín sweaters, your beautifully painted shillelaghs which our people have been so proud to buy and bring back to the States. We love each and every one of you and, ha, ha… I hope that Tipp can win the Triple Crown this year… I *shouldn't* joke like that because I *know* that Tipp will win the Triple Crown this year!

"We love the soft Irish drive!…uh, drizzle, the Blarney Stone outside Dan Murphy's door, the Mountains of Mourne, Galway Bay, the moorlands and the meadows and the 40 shades of green.

"We love your great poets and writers, Yeats and Joyce and Van Gogh. I visited your lovely capital city and was haunted by the words of Joyce, in the Rijksmuseum I thought I heard Rembrandt whispering 'I will arise and go now…'

"Yes this great country is one to be proud of, a constant warning to the Soviets."

29/07/84

Zoo's Who

THE RECENT SIGHTINGS OF a "lioness" on Dublin's Sandymount Strand comes as no surprise to me. Where else would a lioness go *on her holidays???*

The sighting did however surprise those who are aware of the advanced state of industrial relations that now obtain in Dublin Zoo. The zoo's management have so carefully manipulated the media that virtually no-one is aware of the industrial dispute which brought about improved working conditions, one of which was increased holidays; hence the "lioness" at Sandymount.

In the suggestion that the "lioness" in question peered into a car where a couple were behaving like a pair of ani...eh...humans, there is a glorious irony. Doubtless the feline queen of the jungle was making a point about the invasion of privacy which has been the lot for many of the workers in the animal grade at Dublin Zoo.

The trouble began when the zoo, pleading pressure due to the recession, refused the animals full live-in board, a perk that has normally gone with the job. Many animals were disgusted at being sent home for the night.

Representations were made to management who remained intransigent. This caused the immediate implementation of a strict "work to rule" by the animals who claimed that the zoo had a virtual monopoly of the gawking kids market and should improve pay and conditions accordingly.

Management denied this and maintained they were facing stiff opposition for their share of the market from road accidents and dogs copulating, both of which command a wide volume of kids gawking and were less costly to produce and maintain.

The first serious move by the workers occurred when the chimps refused to be rude or unsanitary, always big selling points from the zoo management's point of view.

Then the flamingo's put the foot down — put *both* feet down to be more accurate. The sight of flamingo's with both feet planted firmly in the water was a major source of embarrassment to management. Unused to the hardship of such a sight, it became clear that the public were mere pawns in the tense industrial struggle.

Matters were exacerbated when the Associated Chameleons Union, who were affiliated to the larger Amalgamated Reptiles and Invertebrate union refused point blank to merge — with anything. It was against this background and indeed every background that they defiantly stood out.

Then the hippopotami put in a claim for muddy conditions. They said pointedly that they refused to "lie down and roll over for management" and they would not allow their members or any part of their bodies to wallow in mud without increased remuneration.

Events came to a head when the animals arrived one morning to find themselves locked out. A lock-out at the zoo had been unthinkable and came as a genuine shock to a profession whose main source of livelihood had come from being *locked in!*

In desperation, two lions had rummaged in the bins of the Mirabeau and had been seen afterwards padding proudly O'Connell Bridge with bits of Denis Roussos trailing from their mouths. Inevitably, the bewildered animals became desperate and tragedy was never far away. It came when a bemused and hungry crocodile was apprehended in a city centre store and charged with attempted multiple rape on an expensive handbag collection.

The rhinos revelled in the free time and would frequently head off for a night out on the town chasing loose Land Rovers around Leeson Street.

"You can't beat a nice piece of tailboard," one was heard to remark ribaldly.

Throughout all this the giraffes kept their heads down — pressure on management increased. The kangaroos argued vehemently about the "pound in the pocket" and warned their youngsters never to take money from a stranger again.

Eventually a deal was worked out, including a decrease in productivity from the rabbits in Pet's Corner, an increased herring quota for the seals and full Equity rates for the tigers for their endorsement of a particular brand of petrol.

As all industrial disputes inevitability must, this one ended around a table, where management put their views to the animals, and the chimps put their tea over the director's heads and threw buns at the personnel manager. There were broad smiles all round the table. Normal working practices had been resumed.

27/07/86

Wow! A gutter full of purple prose

THE BRITISH TABLOIDS never cease to amaze. Without fail they manage to churn out headlines which range from the crass to the slyly imbecile. Their capacity to encapsulate any news event in a screaming monosyllabic banner has a certain fascination.

Given the parameters within which they operate, it may be argued that the authors of these abbreviated literary epigrams are indeed some species of genius.

It cannot be gainsaid that the person who managed to reflect on the death of three hundred Argentinean sailors in the South Atlantic with the pithy comment GOTCHA! is without rare gifts. What is the persona which speaks through these headlines?

Is it supposed to be the voice of the reader at which the paper is aimed? Surely that is an injustice to the mass British public? Say what you will about them, I doubt the average British worker possesses the vicious streak which GOTCHA! would imply.

Now on matters relating to royalty, perhaps they are a softer touch for some of the over-the-top gushing prose which is on tap in certain strains of Fleet Street and Wapping.

(Apocryphal question-and-answer No. 1,443 attributed to Larry Gogan's 60-second quiz: LARRY: For what is Fleet Street world-famous? CALLER: Is it the ESB, Larry?)

As one who keeps a wary eye on the tabloids, I looked forward to Thursday morning's offerings from the pocket-size papers. I was not to be disappointed.

The Star (whose masthead had been changed to *Royal Star*, incorporating a crown, for the day) didn't fail me.

"*What a day…*" mused

the front page "*as Andy said to Fergie, WOW.*"

The large reverse-lettering of *Wow* helped that weighty journal to steal a march on its competitors. Quite apart from being smart enough to stick a crown and a Royal prefix in their masthead, the *Royal Star* had managed to produce that most wonderful headline — a three-letter monosyllable.

This is very hard to top unless you can somehow contrive to use only two letters and even the old hands of Fleet Street find it nigh impossible to have a screaming preposition that conveys anything.

(Should any *Tribune* reader feel that this is not so, and feels that he or she can indeed summon up a two-letter heading on the royal wedding, we will unlock the paper's wine cellar and dispatch a bottle of bubbly for the best effort.)

The main story explained all: "*For Prince Andrew there was only one word yesterday to describe Fabulous Fergie...Wow!*"

And the article continues: "*Sarah as usual, also had something to say — Wonderful*". As you can imagine "wonderful" with a full three syllables in it was a definite non-starter for banner status. The piece burbles on about, "*that dress that drew shrieks of delight.*"

There were doubtless more such shrieks outside the palace afterwards when "*Andrew leaned towards his bride and gave her a right royal smacker*".

The *Star* even pointed out that "*Fergie waved with a splendid vim and vigour*".

Guess who gets to scrub the bath in their house? She won't be doing it in the dress that got the *Sun's* punsters labouring to bring forth a masterpiece for their centre page.

"*11.30 special for Westminster, THE TRAIN NOW ARRIVING.*" Of course they had to feature the dress's "*17½ foot train decorated with anchors, hearts, waves and a large A for Andy... but it was the train everyone wanted to catch".*

But enough of this trivia, let's get onto the *Daily Mail* which lent a little gravitas to the proceedings in their editorial: *"in the sight of God and before a congregation of hundreds of millions of television viewers, this man and woman were joined together in Holy Matrimony."* … and wait for this: *"She a wench fit to grace a Tudor revel, with eyes open yet beguiling and hair of beaten copper."*

I mean what can I say, Brian? And the editorial continues… *"He a sailor Prince with a ready grin, who came home from the wars to greet his mother, the Queen, with a rose in his teeth."* Of such stuff are Viennese operettas made.

It all looks promising. There is a fifty-fifty chance that they have their tongues in cheek. There could be a little bit of gentle slagging going on here. A steak of sanity perhaps?

Never mind, tabloid watchers who could become disillusioned by such signs in their favourite comic books can always turn to the *Mirror's* centre page: *THE PRINCE AND MISS BOSSY KNICKERS,* the *Sun's* back page of, *TEDDY FROM EDDIE* or its front page *THEIR BLISS IS A THREE SECOND KISS* for reassurance…

The prince and his bride are now cruising in the Atlantic and being a sailor he will hardly get seasick. Still a glance through the tabloids and he may well throw up.

SCRAP

Scrap Saturday first came on the radio in 1990 but it still seems so clear and so recent —that moment when Dermot, Gerry Stembridge, Pauline McLynn and Owen Roe brought their insane humour into the world. It was a fascinating and dramatic time for Dermot and also for the rest of us — his colleagues, his friends and his family. What Dermot did at the beginning of this decade with the programme became known, at least in some form or another, to everyone in Ireland. It was a highly successful satirical radio show with a huge profile that had people talking about its sketches, its take on current events, and its humour every week. *Scrap* was the thing that Dermot seemed most at ease doing and he obviously enjoyed it, even when things were bad. For him it meant recognition as Dermot Morgan, not as Father Trendy or just 'yer man the comedian', and it lasted by and large until *Father Ted* broke through.

However, though I may only be nineteen, I know that with time you tend to look at things a little more nostalgically than they were in reality. Those four or so years of *Scrap Saturday* were also horrendously frustrating for Dermot. Those were the days when RTÉ had near total control of all broadcasting in Ireland. Commercial radio was just beginning; TV3 was being talked about incessantly as the country's first independent television channel, but it wasn't actually happening yet; and very few independent productions made it onto RTÉ television. As I remember it, this was the time when it eventually became clear to Dermot that he had to look at alternative avenues for success apart from RTÉ. With the limited alternatives at home, he began to put out feelers towards television in England and took his first tentative steps in that direction.

Scrap Saturday was commissioned to fill the 10.00 to 10.30 a.m. slot on a Saturday morning on RTÉ Radio 1. The comedy show *Only Slaggin'* was the immediate predecessor to *Scrap* and Dermot used to listen to it in the way a teacher would listen to a student in an exam. I can still remember driving down Trees Road in Mount Merrion one Saturday morning with him. There's a fantastic view from there of Dublin Bay and it was full of sailing boats and the sun was shining. The radio was on and he was analysing coolly and critically what they were doing on that show. I guess he may have been working out what he'd do if he had a show like that.

He was obviously working on ideas because the next thing I heard was that RTÉ had bought his idea for a series that he would write and, as it turned out, which would go into that slot. The series was known jokingly as *Angelus Rehersal* among Dermot and his friends at first but then became *Scrap Saturday*, a name which I think came from a children's show that was on about the same time called *Scratch Saturday*. The half-hour show was to be produced for RTÉ by Cue Productions, the production company that Dermot had set up to provide a more formal structure for selling his own ideas and work. (The other director was Pat Finn with whom he had been sharing entrepreneurial efforts since college and the unsuccessful ventures of Night Out Entertainments.)

Dermot got together a team of people to work with him to make the show something cohesive, a group that Gerry

Stembridge described as kindred spirits. Gerry was probably the first person Dermot sussed out to see if he could work with him on the writing of the show. The two had known each other for years, although their paths only crossed occasionally. Their first encounter was in 1979 when Dermot was a guest speaker at a debate in UCD. On that evening, Gerry, who was then the auditor of UCD's debating club, the L&H, was in flying form, heckling all the other speakers. Dermot observed him quietly as he savaged the preceding participants. When it came to his turn, Dermot stood up and took Gerry out of it with a brief but effective put-down, preventing any disruption of his speech. God knows what he said, but it worked. That was their first encounter.

Gerry had worked for RTÉ on many occasions over the years. In his time there, he noticed an 'accepted wisdom' amongst some people about Dermot — that he was erratic and all over the place. 'Bad news.' I don't know where this wisdom originated from and I don't know who said it. But it might be a fair guess to say that any view people in RTÉ had of Dermot originated in the aborted *Dermot Morgan Show* in 1983. So when he was first approached by Dermot about working with him on the show, Gerry was a little wary because of what he had heard in those quarters. But I can tell you that Dermot really could be the most persuasive, stubborn man around. He could argue the merits of just about anything with a lot of success. Many is the time I've been annihilated in an argument with him. So Gerry's wariness subsided as he heard what Dermot had to say. Gerry couldn't see what there was to lose. Why not go along with this guy...

Gerry had been doing a television show for RTÉ shortly before Dermot decided to approach him about working on the radio show. It was aimed at teenagers and, I think, was called *Nothing to It*. It was meant to be a kind of self-help guide for teenagers to getting jobs and entering the big, bad world outside school. However, it evolved into a kind of sit-com which based itself loosely around its original aim. I haven't seen it, but apparently Dermot was impressed and decided that not only could he work with Gerry, but also with Pauline McLynn who was also in *Nothing to It*. Actually it was her first television role. Finally Dermot invited Owen Roe, whose vocal talents were well-known in the business, to complete the team.

There's no denying that *Scrap* worked with its mixture of satire, topicality, and commentary on the week's current events. It had qualities that you don't usually find in shows on radio and television. For a start, and I say this as someone who had the fortune to watch it being recorded, although it was very tightly scripted, the scripts were always being updated and improved as events developed. What had been written the previous night was easily changed in seconds to take account of something that had just occurred or, perhaps, to be made a little more energetic than what had been on paper initially. After all, it was written on paper, not in stone. Here's two examples: one day, I think it was the Friday of the second episode, Bobby and I were in the studio watching Dermot, Pauline, Gerry and Owen recording the show. There was a mock ad for a family board game based on the 1916 Rising, complete with some of the most criminally bad Christmas music they could find in the RTÉ archives. Dermot decided to put Bobby and me into the sketch for a more authentic family feel, or maybe just for a laugh. In three, maybe five minutes, the sketch was altered to cater for that. It was a fun experience and an example of how something quite spontaneous could expand the original idea.

Some sketches couldn't be written down completely such as the short but glorious sketch of soccer commentator Jimmy Magee talking dirty to his wife by reciting the names of football players and building up to a climax with a list of Italians. There was not a snowball's chance in hell of writing it all down, so Dermot and Pauline improvised the whole thing, giving the sketch the required level of enthusiasm it needed to work.

Scrap took off pretty quickly as people tuned in to hear what was going to be done with the week's events and who was going to get a kicking. Some people really got a pounding on the show, as the taking-off of their characters expanded beyond caricatures and into the creation of sorts of 'monsters'. Well-known journalist and commentator Eamonn Dunphy was a particular victim of *Scrap*. Dermot had been taking off Eamonn for years here and there, including on his records in the 1980s, but now he had a place from which to launch the Dunphy 'monster' into new realms of madness. And people loved it. They loved it so much that local wags in Dublin gave poor Eamonn a lot of stick about it. There's a story Dermot heard around that time which always cracked him up, which might be told as testimony to the success of the Dunphy sketches. In one of them, the Dunphy character is in the throes of heaping exaggerated praise upon the ex-Leeds United midfielder and former Irish manager, John Giles. It was a take-off of the type of thing that was a regular occurrence with Dunphy in discussions on football programmes, and was taken up, equally regularly, by *Scrap Saturday*. At the end of one such rant on *Scrap*, Dunphy declares his love for Giles and that he is going to have Giles' baby. Shortly after that show, Dunphy is said to have gone into one of his favourite haunts, a bar in a well-known Dublin hotel, and ordered a pint of Guinness. The barman looked up at him and grinned: 'Ah now, Eamonn', he started, 'ye shouldn't be drinking in your condition!' I don't think poor Eamonn was too impressed. Incidentally, by the end of *Scrap*, it transpired that the baby was actually Bono's!

But the most famous 'monster' Dermot created — the one which outgrew any original limits or levels of sanity — was that of the evil, megalomaniacal caricature of the then Taoiseach, Charles Haughey, and his lowly skivvy, Mara — the fictitious incarnation of Haughey's press secretary at the time, P. J Mara. This fictional Mara, masterfully brought to life by Owen Roe, quickly became better known than the real Mara who was not in any way like the slavish, lowly and coarse persona that Dermot and Gerry created for him, but was actually part of Dublin's sophisticated 'café' society.

The notion of Haughey —who presented a public image as a highly cultured, highly imperious political figure — running things with the brutal efficiency of a Godfather became a staple regular on *Scrap* and planted itself firmly into the national consciousness. As time went by and Haughey's political position within his party became untenable, with backbench attempts to remove him eventually succeeding, the *Scrap* incarnation became a half-senile creature living in a dungeon in the depths of his home on Inishmhicilain, Haughey's actual island in the Atlantic. The *Scrap* persona of Mara, his press secretary and downtrodden gofer, stayed always by his side, making sure that things were running well for 'the Boss'. In the third of a series of *Scrap* tapes, *Scrap Charlie* (made specially for the removal of Haughey from office) Mara even looked after him in his dungeon, bringing him his Complan and medicine.

As with all Dermot did, the constraints he may have placed on an idea initially went out the window as he explored more and more potentially riotous avenues of satirical madness. The 'monsters' provided an arena for larger and sometimes wilder theories that Dermot had about Haughey and what he could possibly be up to in his political life. And these 'theories' extended beyond what Haughey alone was up to, to the caricatures of other people; the lowly Mara, or the toadying camp caricature of then Fianna Fail party chairman, Jim Tunney, known on *Scrap* as Biddy Tunney.

By and large the people who were the victims of *Scrap* took it well. Some even enjoyed it: it was almost like a mark of recognition. Fine Gael front-bencher Michael Noonan and sports commentator Jimmy Magee both seemed to revel in it and got on extremely well with Dermot. Actually, Dermot and Michael Noonan met up at one stage in Limerick and had a good time together after a show he did there, which Noonan, as far as I know, went to see. Indeed, when walking up to the church on the day of Dermot's funeral, I noticed Michael Noonan quite unassumingly getting out of his car to attend the service.

What Charles Haughey thought about his 'monster', I don't know. As far as I'm aware he and Dermot only came face to face once, in one of Dublin's best-known and most expensive restaurants, Patrick Guilbaud's. Dermot was being shown to his table when he saw Haughey at another table: he passed by him but was only acknowledged with a silent nod.

On the other side of the coin, some didn't take too kindly to being featured on the show at all. The Fianna Fáil Senator Donie Cassidy was for a while a favourite target of Dermot's. For anyone who doesn't know much about him, he's known for sporting what can only be described as a particularly obvious toupee. In one of the shows, there was a reference made to Cassidy driving in a cabriolet, 'his hair blowing in the wind behind him, but he was too embarrassed to pick it up'. Senator Cassidy took offence at this and made contact with Dermot and Gerry through his solicitor. From a letter I found from Cassidy's solicitors, they even demanded a tape of the offending piece. As far as Dermot was concerned it was a joke and it baffled him that someone could react like that. That said, it also amused the hell out of him: he was almost relishing the thought of a huge, farcical case about the whole thing in front of the High Court. It would have been fabulous coverage for the show, *á la* Howard Stern or someone like that. The week after those representations were made, Pauline made an 'apology' to Senator Cassidy at the end of the show in her official RTÉ voice, which was something she took a great amount of pleasure in doing. 'We now accept that Senator Cassidy's hair is his own,' she announced in that 'official' voice. 'We have seen the receipt.'

Scrap, though, wasn't all fun and games. I can remember Dermot often getting quite frustrated by the way RTÉ wanted to oversee the show, and what he and the others were doing down in that studio on a Friday morning. In the beginning, RTÉ would request copies of the scripts of the shows at an early stage of the week, even though it was a topical show and the scripts would more than likely change right up to the last minute in the studio. They presumably made an assumption that the show was read off a script prepared well in advance, like in radio drama, something that simply didn't happen with topical satire like *Scrap*. I guess comedy in general doesn't work along the lines of drama anyway, as it is more spontaneous. That seeming lack of understanding on RTÉ's part of what the *Scrap* team was doing was a point of tension between them and the station.

An early shot of Dermot in one of his best-known guises, Father Trendy, 1980.

A routine from the running sketches of the Mexican dictator from *The Dermot Morgan Show,* 1983.

Dermot in his various guises as a Tour de France cyclist, Garda Síochána, and Ireland soccer player.

As Ronald Reagan, from the video of *Thank You Very Much, Mr Eastwood.*

The GAA fanatic
who regularly
wielded a hurley
stick mid-diatribe,
from *The Live Mike.*

Posing as Barry McGuigan, for the launch of the hit record *Thank You Very Much, Mr Eastwood.*

(photo courtesy of Maxwell's Photo Agency)

Jim, the rugger-fanatic, waxes lyrical.

The cover shot from *Daddy's in Deutschland*, the hit-single of the European Championships, 1988.

Dermot's cheesy 1980s-style TV presenter character 'Eddie Van Dringen' accosts an actress posing as an American U2 fan, near the Windmill Lane studios in Dublin, 1988.

The famous Flamingos in their pink jerseys, including Ray Treacy (standing, far left), Dave Fanning (standing, far right), Michael Redmond (standing, second from right), Peter Redmond (standing, middle) and Pat Finn (kneeling, second from right)

The Scrap Saturday team. (from left) Dermot, Pauline McLynn, Gerry Stembridge and Owen Roe, 1990.

At the Q Magazine awards with Ruud Gullit.

'... and another thing...' Dermot with Gerry Stembridge in Kites Restaurant after a gig in the Olympia, 1993.

At the Jacob's Radio Awards, 1994, with his partner Fiona (far left), sister Denise and brother-in-law Declan.

Fr Ted and friends, 1996.

Sporadic disagreements over what went into the show, and what they perceived to be RTÉ's attitude to them, pissed them off. How RTÉ wanted the operation to be run and how Dermot and Gerry and the *Scrap* team wanted it to be run were largely different. So they took what Gerry describes as 'an arrogant decision' not to play ball with RTÉ. In one argument with RTÉ over the content of a show, Dermot and Gerry stormed out of the studio and went over to the RTÉ canteen, where they remained most of that Friday morning. The rest of the team joined them in solidarity until they were finally coaxed back into the studio. Also, I remember a strike by technicians in RTÉ during one of the series affecting the broadcast of that week's show, which, I assume, was also frustrating for Dermot. He and Gerry decided to record the show for that week in Reelgood studios in the centre of Dublin to avoid the strike and get the show on air. Although they got the show recorded RTÉ wouldn't broadcast it because of the delicate negotiations in resolving the strike.

There were two series of *Scrap Saturday* broadcast on RTÉ radio between 1990 and 1992. In that time it became a cult series, won a Jacob's Award in the annual Irish broadcasting awards, and RTÉ received a certain amount of kudos for broadcasting it. Negotiations began on commissioning a third series of the show but RTÉ decided to discontinue it. The decision came completely out of the blue: I don't think Dermot expected it at all. One moment the show looked like it would have another run, the details were being negotiated. The next moment the show was no more. It seemed at the time, and still seems, to be inexplicable. Why take off a perfectly good show at the height of its success? Maybe the whole thing was just too much hassle for RTÉ, having to deal with those difficult bastards, Morgan, Stembridge, McLynn and Roe. Maybe they were under pressure from higher powers to end it, as some journalists suggested after Dermot died. (I heard that a tridentine bishop from Offaly performed an exorcism on RTÉ to remove Gay Byrne and *Scrap*...)

Naturally, our father was very upset by its shelving. He had put so much hard work into bringing about this series, and had brought it to levels of success unheard of for RTÉ comedy, an area in which the station's track record was more than a little patchy. There have been numerous rumours over the years as to why *Scrap Saturday* was shelved. Many are conspiracy theories — that RTÉ freaked out at this crowd taking shots at their employers, the politicians. However it's more than likely that when they were looking at *Scrap* and wondering whether or not they should commission a third series, they looked on it as another season of hassle.

So the series ended peremptorily and was launched instead into Irish broadcasting legend, where it still holds a special place. But it didn't totally end there: Dermot and Gerry had already brought out one *Scrap Saturday* cassette, *Scrap, The Tapes*, and now decided to bring out two more specially written cassettes. The first, *Scrap Annual*, was based around the fictitious notion of Charles Haughey's New Years' party after an attempt by some in Fianna Fáil to remove him from the leadership. The final, and definitely the best, *Scrap Charlie*, was released after Haughey was finally ousted from the Fianna Fáil leadership: it plays with him as a senile prisoner, with shades of King Lear ranting out on the moors, while Mara tries to write his biography.

Scrap finally came to an end in February 1997 in the Andrew's Lane Theatre in Dublin with a live performance of new material for the launch of the new independent radio station, Radio Ireland, now Today FM. It was performed on the day of the station's launch in front of a capacity audience in the small theatre, many of whom, ironically, were from RTÉ. It demonstrated again the creative power of the series, a power that Dermot, Gerry, Pauline and Owen were all well aware of, and revealed it in its finest light — live, spontaneous and unbridled madness.

After *Scrap* ended, Dermot really concentrated on stand-up, whilst continuing to plug away at other opportunities. He was exploring the possibility of doing something in England, having discussions with commissioning editors in Channel 4. However, his dealings with RTÉ had one final chance for success in 1993/4 in the shape of a show with a format similar to that of BBC's *Have I Got News For You?* to be called *Newshounds*. It meant the chance of another collaboration with Gerry Stembridge as well as people like Fiona Looney, Anne Marie Hourihane, the late Gerry MacNamara (who was a collaborator of Fiona Looney's) and a young producer, Philip Kampff. RTÉ seemed to be very much in favour of doing the series and they began the process of producing a show. Dermot was delighted. Maybe this would be his chance to get a television show, in which he would have a very central role as the presenter. It was soon in an advanced state of development and two pilots had been made. As Fiona Looney explains: 'There were meant to be two pilots done and then it would go out the following week and the first pilot was very good... everyone [on the show] was happy with the first one.'

So things looked good. The first pilot had been excellent; though the second, although quite respectable, wasn't as good as the first. But both had given them enough time to see exactly what was and wasn't working and they had gotten the show to a level good enough for broadcasting. There was some risqué, but extremely funny, ad-libbing on the pilots, as Fiona Looney remembers: 'There were a couple of corking jokes in it, like the idea of Michael D.

[Higgins, then Minister for the Arts and Culture] hiring leather-bound queens as chauffeurs.'

Things looked set for the show to go on air. But then RTÉ intervened and asked to delay the broadcast for a week so they could maybe do a third pilot. Two days later, at the very last minute, the show was shelved. No ifs, ands or buts. It was cancelled. The producer, Philip Kampff, had seemingly heard about the decision when it was passed along as if it was second-hand information. All the others found out subsequently, I think, from Philip. Everyone was upset. Shortly after they heard the news, Dermot, Philip and Gerry marched into the office of the RTÉ senior executive who was the controller of programmes, and vented their anger at him. Apparently the executive just sat there impassively, listening to what they had to say.

Dermot was totally shattered, actually broken by what RTÉ had decided to do. I can remember him being possessed with anger, frustration and despair. He did what I always remember him doing at times of major disappointment. He would get in the car and just drive. Sometimes he went down to the Pigeon House, to the mouth of Dublin harbour where you can walk right out into the bay to the Poolbeg lighthouse. Other times he would just drive around anywhere. And he also watched the film *The Godfather*, another thing he did when feeling down, and thought up elaborate schemes about how to get even: that usually cheered him up. (Thoughts of revenge often cheered him up in such circumstances. On another occasion after RTÉ had knocked him down, he came across an excellent cartoon of one of the station's executives and spent a happy day trying to figure out how he could have it printed on toilet rolls!)

What always amazed me, though, was how quickly Dermot bounced back, even after such terrible disappointments as *Scrap* and *Newshounds*. It wasn't long before he was again scribbling down a million-and-one ideas for other projects. Some of them he simply forgot about, others he explored a little more, like his idea for a novel about the German football manager Franz Beckenbauer being kidnapped, to be called *The Kaiser Conspiracy*. I think it was to be a spoof of Frederick Forsyth-type books like *The Day Of The Jackal*, although Dermot loved that novel.

Around that time his old friend, Denis Waterman, was in Dublin in a production of *Jeffrey Bernard Is Unwell* at the Olympia Theatre. The two got together and had one of those epic sessions in which you could end up in just about any place by the end of the night. By the end of that particular night, they were in the Westbury Hotel where Denis was staying. Gerry Adams had just been allowed to speak on television for the first time in Ireland. Denis turned to Dermot and said to him, 'Well, I always knew the IRA would get their slot on RTÉ before you.'

The early 1990s had been filled with ups-and-downs for him. *Scrap* had been a success; there had been the disappointments of its sudden end and of the *Newshounds* decision; but his stand-up was going really well. And, in November 1993, he had another son, our littlest brother, Ben. But that period of professional highs and inordinately cruel lows showed him that ultimately he'd have to look elsewhere than RTÉ. There were some prospects in commercial radio in Ireland and he was still trying to explore what might be on offer in broadcasting in England.

For a while he had an early morning radio show on the Dublin commercial station, 98FM, called *Guten Morgan* which opened with over-the-top German marching music —

just the thing to get you going in the morning. I can still remember being late for school from time to time because of listening to it. The format was a mix of chat and music and it was quite successful, especially since most of it was chat. That was particularly good fun when he had people like journalists Sam Smyth and Paddy Murray on, friends of his with whom he could engage in any amount of madness.

And then there was, as always, stand-up and touring.

SCRAP

The Scripts

The following extracts come mainly from the three tapes that were released following the initial success of Scrap *and the subsequent shelving of it by RTÉ:* Scrap Saturday: the Tapes, Scrap Annual *and the final,* Scrap Charlie. *Two of the sketches come from the last-ever* Scrap *show,* Scrap Ireland, *which was performed in front of a live audience in Dublin's Andrew's Lane theatre for the launch in February 1997 of the new commercial radio station, Radio Ireland, now called Today FM.*

President Robinson's Inauguration

This sketch was originally broadcast as part of the first series in 1990 at the time Mary Robinson was inaugurated as the seventh President of Ireland and the first woman to hold the position. The sketch was also on the first tape brought out from the success of Scrap Saturday, *entitled* Scrap Saturday: the Tapes, *in the section called* The Road to the Red Cow Inn. *In the sketch, Mara and Haughey are watching Robinson's inauguration ceremony and it's pretty clear that someone's not too happy about her hogging all the limelight...*

(*National Anthem playing in the background*)

HAUGHEY: PJ why is that woman getting all the attention?

MARA: Jaysus, Boss she's the President. We have to let her have centre stage, it's her day.

HAUGHEY: But I'm...

MARA: I know.

HAUGHEY: Her escort is twenty shagging motorcycles, what do I get? Neanderthal Man, straight out of Templemore in a greasy anorak.

MARA: Ah, Boss the Branch are looking after you.

HAUGHEY: What's happening back at the office?

MARA: Ah, yer man Harris was on again. He's desperate for a gig.

HAUGHEY: You can tell him to F... Tell him where to go.

MARA: Ah I will Boss, but he worked for herself didn't he... he says that sex appeal is the secret of success.

HAUGHEY: I know that, of course. I don't need advisors telling me that. I have sex appeal, that's why I will stay leader. Who else has it? Flynn?

(PJ laughing in the background)

HAUGHEY: Collins? Ah she's a fine women our President. Very good for the National image to have a women president. Makes the Europeans think we're a modern society. Go down well in Bonn, should be good for a few more Deutchmarks or ECUs or whatever's going.

MARA: Oh God it will Boss, yes.

HAUGHEY: Apart from which... she has nice legs.

MARA: Ah now Boss.

HAUGHEY: (leeringly) Very short skirts.

MARA: Ah stop, you're not over Maggie yet, now don't be getting all hot and bothered now she is the President.

HAUGHEY: Typical Mara, you see the President, I see the woman.

The Adviser

This also comes from the first series and can be found on the same tape as the previous sketch, under the section called Sex, Lies and Audiotape. *Its origins lay in the controversy over a leading Irish travel agent's ad campaign showing a rear shot of a woman's unclothed bum staring out at the world. Haughey and Mara debate the finer merits of Haughey's tourism adviser and head of the same travel agency, Gillian Bowler...*

HAUGHEY: PJ

PJ: ah... Yes Boss

HAUGHEY: *[barking]*: What the hell is going on?

PJ: What?

HAUGHEY: I pay you to keep in touch with what's going on among my people. You're not doing your job.

PJ: Oh yes Boss, I always do, ah... a robin can not sing from the bough or a blade of grass bend in the breeze but you are aware of it.

HAUGHEY: So, how come you don't tell me the most important news of the week?

PJ: Hmmm... oh don't worry about the old Lenihan book, we have that dealt with.

HAUGHEY: No Mara! The most important news of the week. I have a certain adviser...

PJ: Oh yes Boss. Ahh... Gillian ehh...

HAUGHEY: Gillian Bowler!

PJ: Oh yes.

HAUGHEY: Fine woman

PJ: Oh...oh... she has a fine set of teeth Boss, wouldn't like to share an apple with her. Ha, ha!

HAUGHEY: Silence Mara. How dare you speak about her like that. She's an adviser.

PJ: Well of course Boss, you have lots of advisors. Taoiseachs always do.

HAUGHEY: Lots of advisers but all grey suits and grey minds and grey hairs. My advisers are an elegy to grey. Cronin – there's only so much about Myles and Arts Council and culture even I can take, and, oh yeah, the Secretary of *my* Department, Ó Huigínn. Speaks every language under the sun. All singing, all thinking mandarin with as much real colour as Larry Gogan's hair. He speaks every language under the sun except the language of love, the *lingua franca* of the loins. None of them make me feel the way she does when she's in here... she's spring PJ, she's little animals gambolling... little birds singing their song from the meadow, while I'm like an ox in the back field, on the tread mill of duty. She makes me want to toss off my yoke...

Dealing with a Savage Leader

First series and same tape again. Following a disturbing phone call from a man about his sheep on a parody of the RTÉ phone-in radio programme, 'Ask About Pets', a concerned Bertie Ahern rings in to ask about what to do with a savage leader. The sketch followed Haughey's sacking of Brian Lenihan, his Presidential candidate, from his cabinet after Lenihan became embroiled in controversy during the election campaign. But it wasn't just Haughey's Fianna Fáil party that had leadership problems...

RADIO PRESENTER: Hello caller you're on the air

FIRST CALLER: Hello, ah, I have this sheep, she's quite healthy now, but one or two problems have cropped up lately.

2ND RADIO PRESENTER: Yeah, I'll take this one Peter. Tell us, caller, have you dosed her against the Eightclausdriddell diseases now, you have?

CALLER: She's as clean as a whistle now, lots of wool and the usual features, black face, quite stunning actually, and the hooves and the eight nipples very firm, beautifully pointed now and they're grand.

2ND RADIO PRESENTER: Do you think it might be Mangemite or Sucking Lice or something like that.

CALLER: Well I wouldn't know about that now, but she's a great sheep to handle and there's not a bother on her at all, but she was a bit reluctant about going in the dip the first time so I just stripped off and jumped in with her and...

RADIO PRESENTER *(cutting in):*

Yeah, well we'll have to look at that later...We have another caller on the line.

2ND CALLER:

Eh... Hello. I heard someone on earlier about a tame leader, we have the exact opposite problem, eh... we have a vicious leader. Earlier last week there, he went for two of the candidates in the presidential election.

RADIO PRESENTER:

And who did he go for Bertie? Bertie isn't it?

BERTIE:

That's right. He went for two of the candidates, a woman and a man, both very nice people, but eh... he went for both of them.

RADIO PRESENTER:

And where was this Bertie?

BERTIE:

It was above in the national stadium, eh... now we had another animal it's a St Padraig, eh... that went for that unfortunate woman Mrs. Robinson and there's some evidence he has rabies, so err... we are, like, afraid we're going to have to put him down, but at least we knew this was his form like...

RADIO PRESENTER:

Yes

142

BERTIE: But we're now more worried about the savage leader, it's kind of a cross between a King Charles and a Greensetter, it looks like a pug, err... now we tried to put him down... err... three times before but, err... the injections didn't work and now there isn't a vet in the country will handle the job.

RADIO PRESENTER *(concerned)*:

Is he particularly vicious Bertie?

BERTIE: Ah yeah he's gone for a few people and one of our favourite pets, em... we had a curly haired Tánaiste, lovely quiet old fool, very faithful – do anything you ask him. But last week the savage leader turned on him, you know, it's like after all these years, you know, there was blood everywhere.

RADIO PRESENTER: Shame. Next Caller.

3RD CALLER: Hello...

RADIO PRESENTER: Hello, who's that?

3RD CALLER: Excuse me I didn't interrupt you!

RADIO PRESENTER: No you're on the air.

3RD CALLER *(indignantly)*:

I know I'm on the air, I've known that for the last five seconds.

RADIO PRESENTER: Well what's your question?

3RD CALLER:	Well, my problem, men in the house, is that we're keeping a tame leader.

3RD CALLER: Well, my problem, men in the house, is that we're keeping a tame leader.

RADIO PRESENTER: Ah... How old is he?

3RD CALLER: He's about 42.

RADIO PRESENTER: And what do you think might be the problem, caller?

3rd CALLER: Well, the problem is that we got him because we wanted him to mind the sheep and he's turned out to be a bit wayward. He isn't aggressive enough.

RADIO PRESENTER: And have you considered having him... him castrated?

3RD CALLER: Ah...indeed we did, but when we looked we couldn't find any...

RADIO PRESENTER: Next caller.

Bearing Gifts

This extract is from the second tape, Scrap Annual, *and contains original material that was never broadcast on the radio. The plot of the tape surrounds Haughey's first Christmas party since an unsuccessful attempt to oust him as leader. The party has reached the stage where gifts must be offered to him...*

CROWD (*singing*):   Oh...Charlie we love you!!!

HAUGHEY: P.J.

MARA: Yes Boss...yes...

HAUGHEY: Tell these em... morons... supporters ... that I'm very moved and ask them what presents they've brought me... and they'd better be good.

MARA (*clearing his throat*):

Everybody... the Boss is well pleased with your greeting... he is very moved... but of course he will not be moved...ha, ha.

HAUGHEY (*barking*):   MARA!

MARA: Just a little joke, just a little joke... You may now come to him with whatever little offerings that you have.

HAUGHEY: BIG... big offerings.

MARA: Oh yes Boss, err... Whatever you consider appropriate to offer such a great man. Now, come forward now.

CATHAL DALY: Sir Haughey... I say to you the Spiritual covenants of Catholics from every city in the land...

HAUGHEY: Thank you Cardinal... move along now won't you... Ah... Bertie, my little godson Bartholomew.

BERTIE: Err... hello Sir... I, I can only offer you d'd'wealth of the nation, but not for ever, for a certain time frame.

HAUGHEY: My lifetime perhaps... Bertie my old brown son?

BERTIE: At least Sir...whatever you're having yourself, m...mine's a Bass.

HAUGHEY: Good Bertie, very witty. Paul McGuiness, good to see you again.

McGUINNESS: I'm sure it is CJ... for such a great occasion, a great gesture. I'll give you my clients. Four young geniuses CJ, use them at your pleasure.

HAUGHEY: ...great...err...hope they can sing 'Arise and Follow Charlie'. PJ?

MARA: Yes Boss.

HAUGHEY: ... the little blonde lad...sit up here on my knee sonny.

LARRY MULLEN: ... no man.

HAUGHEY *(dissapointed)*:

There's nothing wrong...two men... oh well...

LARRY MULLEN:	... not into it man!
HAUGHEY:	Err... bring him up to my room, I'll get him to beat a rhythm out for me later.
MARA:	Sure thing, Boss. Sure thing!
HAUGHEY:	Eamonn, what can you do for your master?
DUNPHY:	I'm prepared to fawn on you in the *Indo* every week. I'll apply the full weight of my pen in your defence. I'll toady and dance to your tune. I'm prepared to make myself look ridiculous in the eyes of the world.
HAUGHEY:	Yes but what new things will you do?

Naming the Deer

Scrap Charlie was brought out just after the final and successful attempt to remove Haughey as leader of Fianna Fáil. The tape shows him bewildered and confused, exiled to his island in the Atlantic as reality slips away, whilst Mara tries to piece together the official biography of his leader. Haughey has slipped outside with his shotgun to name the deer he wants to shoot...

(Blizzard effects)

MARA: Boss, Boss, where are you? Come in out of that, you'll catch a death of cold.

HAUGHEY (*confused*): Hello? What?

MARA: PJ, Boss, it's me PJ. Come back into the house Boss, I've got some lovely fresh straw in your cell... your room... your suite, Boss.

HAUGHEY: I've been looking at the deer gambolling. I'm giving them names you know.

MARA: Ah... that's lovely, that's a lovely idea Boss. Names like Rudolf, Fanta, Bambi?

HAUGHEY: No, No, I'm calling that... see that one there... Albert, and see that's Garret and see that one over there with the funny head?

MARA: Yeah...

HAUGHEY:	That's Dessie.
MARA:	Ah... I see.
HAUGHEY *(dreamily)*:	We might go hunting tomorrow eh... Maureen.
MARA:	No, it's PJ Boss, Maureen's the other one... the love of your life Boss.
HAUGHEY:	Oh really yeah...looking at those little deer gamboling I remember my own salad days of youth and joy. Though of course a stallion would probably fit the picture more.

Meeting U2

This again is from Scrap Charlie. *It shows the often black streak that* Scrap *frequently displayed in moments of madness. This sketch involves the hapless U2 drummer...*

HAUGHEY *[shouting]*: Mara! How often have you had me on the cover of *Time* Magazine*?* How often?

MARA: Umm...

HAUGHEY: Never! You have never had me on the cover of *Time*.

MARA: Very true.

HAUGHEY: And I pick up *Time* and who do I see on it?

MARA: U2

HAUGHEY: No not me too, those two, those four. Four gurriers, whipper-snappers, four tuneless gobshites and they... they grace the cover of *Time* Magazine.

MARA: Yeah, but it's rock music Boss, that's different.

HAUGHEY: They're on the cover of *Time* Magazine Mara – get them in here, we need a reception.

[Mara voice-over: As usual we had a reception]

HAUGHEY:	Which one is that?
MARA:	That's the Edge Boss.
HAUGHEY:	I told you I don't want her here.
MARA:	No THE Edge, Boss, yeah, he's the guitar player.
HAUGHEY:	Hmm... and why is he wearing a scarf?
MARA:	Well...
HAUGHEY:	My mother used to wear a scarf and she wasn't in a rock band. Which one is that?
MARA:	Bono
HAUGHEY:	Hmm... good Latin name. Oh and who's this young fella? *(Leeringly)* Come here to me... tell me, son what do you play?
YOUNG FELLA:	Ahh... I play the skins man.
HAUGHEY:	The skins man.
YOUNG FELLA:	The drummer, that's what I am, that's what I am, I was always gonna be a drummer you know.
HAUGHEY:	Have you always worn an earring?
YOUNG FELLA:	Huh?
HAUGHEY:	Smashing young fella, sit up there on my knee, come over here to me.
YOUNG FELLA:	Uhh... hold on, take it easy...
HAUGHEY:	Nothing wrong... take it easy...

YOUNG FELLA: I'll tell you what I thought about George man but I'm not into it OK!

HAUGHEY: You could come to the island and live with the deer – after all drummers are a dying species. I mean there was Keith Moon and the fella from the Beach Boys.

YOUNG FELLA: Look man, take it easy.

HAUGHEY: You'd be safer on the island. We could breed a herd of drummers.

YOUNG FELLA: I'm not into it man, take it easy, I'm not into it...

The Missing Million

This is from Scrap Ireland *and is probably the most prophetic of all the work that was produced for* Scrap. *It concerns the scandals about a senior Fianna Fáil politician taking payments from supermarket tycoon, Ben Dunne, and shows Haughey ringing Mara to find out where the money has gone. But Mara's now no longer his skivvy...*

(A receptionist's office. Her phone rings, she answers.)

HAUGHEY *(growls)*:   MARA!

RECEPTIONIST: Yes, MARA here.

HAUGHEY: You don't' sound like Mara to me. What happened, old friend? Did you have them lopped off, did you? Hmm? Never thought of you as a gelding. A faithful old cart-horse, yes. But a gelding? Never!

RECEPTIONIST: I'm sorry you must have the wrong number.

HAUGHEY: I want Mara!

RECEPTIONIST: Err... well that's what you have — MARA: Public Relations Corporate Media Consultant.

HAUGHEY: I want Mara himself – MARA!... MARA!

RECEPTIONIST: Oh, I'll see if **MR** Mara is available.

HAUGHEY:	Mr. Mara! Who the hell is *Mr.* Mara?
	[Receptionist knocks on Mara's office door]
RECEPTIONIST:	I'm sorry Mr. Mara. There's some old man on the phone, says he wants to talk to you.
MARA:	Oh Jaysus, that'll be Tony Ryan, what did his young fella get up to now? Or who has he got up to more likely.
RECEPTIONIST:	No, no, sir he says his name is Haw-hee.
MARA:	Haw-hee, Haw-hee, no, no, where have I heard that name? Ah Jaysus – not yer man! Not the old...How did he get my number?
RECEPTIONIST:	He sounded like he really needed to talk to someone.
MARA:	Well, tell him to call the Samaritans.
RECEPTIONIST:	He sounded a bit insistent.
MARA:	Haughey 'a bit insistent' – ah... Jaysus, that's like saying a Piranha's a bit peckish, or Fergie's a bit ugly! All right put him on.
HAUGHEY:	MARA! Get over here now! And who is that girl who left me waiting? What kind of secretary is the civil service recruiting now?
MARA:	The civil service, ah... no, no, no, she works for me, in the private business. Oh a little smasher. Jaysus,

a skirt halfway up her, her armpits!
A cracker!

HAUGHEY: Oh right, I forgot hmm... civil service secretaries are all bow-wows.

MARA: Ah, now, you can't say that these days.

HAUGHEY: I can say whatever I like. I want to see you!

MARA: No-can-do Charlie. Now let's see, breakfast meeting tomorrow 9 a.m., 10 o'clock hmm... working lunch with hmm... 1p.m., 3 o'clock hmm... oh I might have a window on the 18th... of November...

HAUGHEY *(shouts!)*: What?

MARA: 2001!

HAUGHEY: I know the window I have for you and you'll go out of it: you're forgetting who I am.

MARA: Everybody's forgotten who you are!

HAUGHEY: I'm The Boss... Your Chief... Leader... Il Duce...

MARA: Oh yes, Boss... Chief... Leader... *(chuckles)*

HAUGHEY: Hmm... now Mara , there's talk some senior Fianna Fáil figure received £1.1 million. Where is it Mara? Where's it gone?

MARA: Did you try your piggy bank?

HAUGHEY *(barks)*: How dare you!

MARA: Ah... come on, Charlie!

(Receptionist returns to the room)

RECEPTIONIST: Mr. Mara, Sir, Smurfit on line one, Dermot Desmond on line three.

MARA: Oh right, yeah... Anyway I'm sorry I have to make another call. I'll get back to you on that... some time.

HAUGHEY *(pleads)*: MARA... MARA... PJ... *Mein treuer...* *PJ...* MAARAaaa...

From Scrap Ireland 1997

This is also from Scrap Ireland *and features another favourite target of the* Scrap *team, Michael Noonan. He was Minister for Health at the time and found himself having to deal with the Hepatitis C scandal over the Blood Bank infecting thousands of women over two decades. Noonan's defence was along the following lines ...*

	(In a Church, sounds of people praying. Noonan enters the confessional.)
NOONAN:	Bless me Father for I have sinned. It's been at least one Dáil session since my last confession. Father, I stole six-pence from Mammy's purse.
PRIEST:	I see.
NOONAN:	I mean that is the view of some people in this church, but the facts are that first of all Mammy shouldn't have left her purse where she did, and secondly this purse had been lying there long before I took over as her son. There were other sons before me, when the problem arose in the first place.
PRIEST:	You must take responsibility for your own sins and not blame others.
NOONAN:	Right... well I apologise if I appear to be insensitive to Mammy on this matter.
PRIEST:	Right... continue.

NOONAN:	And I err... swore... I used the Lord's name in vain.
PRIEST:	Tell me now, did you swear much?
NOONAN:	Well of course... The issue of swearing is a complicated one and an emotive one for a lot of people in this community, so I don't want to pre-empt any inquiry into that whole area.
PRIEST:	Now, did you or did you not swear? It's a simple question, yes or no?
NOONAN *(shouts)*:	I didn't interrupt you! 'Tis easy for the member of the clergy now sitting on the other side of the grill to come into this box and hurl allegations and accusations without the responsibility for my soul – 'tis easy to be the hurler in the ditch.
PRIEST:	Right, well continue.
NOONAN:	... and uh... Father I...
PRIEST:	What?
NOONAN:	... I played with myself.
PRIEST:	Well there's nothing wrong with that, if there were no other boys around. What could you do but play with yourself?
	(Long pause)
NOONAN:	No... I mean I... masturbated.
PRIEST *(appalled)*:	You masturbated!!
NOONAN:	It isn't as simple a matter as that you know. 'Tis easy for the member of the clergy to sit on the other side of that grill and accuse me. The fact of the matter is that this masturbation

started with previous sinners... and I'm prepared to have a full Tribunal of Inquiry into this. Questions need to be asked. Who left the *Playboy* open on my desk, disguised as *St Martin's Monthly News*? Why instead of religious information, did I find 'Miss January' lolling in her birthday suit wearing a nurse's cap? These are questions that need to be addressed.

PRIEST: Well if you are in all humility...

NOONAN: ... well, I wouldn't say humility.

PRIEST: ...heartily... truly...

NOONAN: Heartily might be an overstatement.

PRIEST *(tentatively)*: ... and abjectly sorry

NOONAN: The member of the clergy on the other side of the grill is putting words in my mouth!

PRIEST: You can say three Our Fathers, three Hail Marys and three Glory Bes.

NOONAN: You can say what you like...

PRIEST *(exasperatedly)*: Are you or are you not sorry for your sins?

NOONAN: Well certainly I regret any inadvertent six-pence stealing, swearing or masturbation that may have been carried out by previous sinners who held office.

PRIEST: And what about the penance I've just given you?

NOONAN: I'll set up a commission to look into it. God Bless!

The National Question — Is it 1916 or a Quarter-Past-Seven?

Performed in the style of I Love Lucy, *all the characters have American accents, except for James (Jimmy) Connolly, whom the Americans mistake for the comedian Billy Connolly — hence the Scottish accent.*

	[Opening fanfare]
MC:	And now it's comedy time, with the 1916 gang in *I Love Pearsie*.
	[Doorbell]
Female Voice:	Oh, I wonder who that could be? Maybe it's Dev? Ah, ah he'll be down at Boland's Mills again. It's more likely Pearsie.
	[Door opening]
Female Voice:	Why it's Pearsie.
	[Cheering and applause from studio audience]
Female voice:	Hello Padraic.
Padraic Pearse:	Hi 'ya
Female Voice:	For a moment then I thought it would be Dev.
Pearse:	Uh, uh, you know Dev.

Female & Pearse:	He'll be down at Boland's Mills again!
Pearse:	Say would you guys like to go to the Post Office?
Female Voice:	Easter Sunday, go to the Post Office? OK, but what's happening?
Pearse:	A rising!
	(Cheers from studio audience)
Female Voice:	Oh no, not another rising!
Pearse:	Well why not, for crying out loud. Everyone will be there.
Female voice.	Not Dev.
Pearse.	You're right!
Together:	He'll be down at Boland's Mills again!
	(Canned laughter)
Female voice:	But Pearsie, remember what happened the last time.
Pearse:	It will be different this time.
Female voice:	You and your big ideas. Last time we went for a day out to Howth you had to go and spoil it all by taking those stupid rifles off the Asgard...
	(Cheers from studio audience)
Female voice:	... meanwhile Roger got into trouble with that stupid submarine off Barna Strand... and all those things they said about him in court... *sniffle...*

and now... *sniffle*... now you want a rising!

Pearse: Oh there, there.

Female Voice: Oh Padraic, every time you do this sort of thing we get into trouble with General French.

[More canned laughter]

Pearse: Dev's not worried about getting into trouble and neither am I.

Female Voice: Of course Dev's not worried, he's got American citizenship.

[Doorbell]

Pearse: Hey, cheer up, that will be Uncle James from Gorballs. Hi Jimmy

Connolly: *[in Scottish accent]*
See you Padraic.

[Cheer from audience]

Pearse. Ladies and Gentleman, why it's Jimmy Connolly!

Connolly. Now see hear... this Dublin's a strange sort of place. Oh aye, people playing with their proclamations and that, know what I mean, I just wanted to buy a stamp at the Post Office, the next thing you know I've half the bloody British Empire trying to molocate me. Gun boats on the Liffey, the bloody lot!

[Doorbell]

Female voice. Wonder who that is?

Connolly.	Well it'll not be Dev.
All three.	'cause he'll be down at Bolland's Mills again.
	[Door opening]
Female voice.	Why if it isn't Yeatsie!
	Ladies and Gentlemen, would you like to hear a poem everyone?
From the Crowd.	Give us a poem Billy.
Connolly.	Oh aye, give us a poem and don't be hanging around like a fart in a phone box.
Yeats.	I'll write it in a verse: McDonagh and McBride, and Connolly and Pearse. Now and in time to be whenever green is worn, Are changed, changed utterly. A terrible beauty is born.
Female voice.	Oh, Billy that was sweet, a terrible beauty. More like a terrible pity that that's all we have time for this week.
	[Theme music]
MC.	And *I Love Pearsie* was recorded in front of a dead audience and is now playing nightly in Belfast, Crossmaglen, Armagh, Derry...
Female voice.	...and Newry! Bye, bye folks!
Pearse.	Bye, bye
Connolly.	See you!

Black Humour

Stand-up had been an extremely hard slog for Dermot in the 1980s, but it was something he had had to do to make a living when RTÉ wasn't an option for him, and he had got by somehow. In the 1990s though, the situation had changed and Dermot was able to find an audience as a stand-up comedian. *Scrap* had taken off and established him as a well-known name and there were also comedy clubs popping up around the country. Other venues were also ready to book stand-up acts because of the growing demand to see good comedy, especially in Dublin and Cork where a good few venues had comedy nights during the week. Dermot was no longer one of a small minority trying to operate on a wild frontier.

When Dermot wasn't in the studio recording *Scrap*, you could at least guess that he was doing a gig somewhere. When *Newshounds* was shot down, he was still touring. Come to think of it, stand-up is the one thing that Dermot did continuously during the 1990s, and it won him one of Ireland's annual National Entertainment Awards.

The kind of touring Dermot did around the time of *Scrap* involved just him and his material, which he had perfected over the years. That was it; he kept things simple. It was done very much on a basis of the demand that was now there for him. He used to call it at the time the 'Nilfisk tour' (hoovering up the cash) and he would say to me 'Pays your school fees, son'. However, when *Scrap* met its premature demise, and *Newshounds* suffered a similar fate, stand-up had to pay for more than school fees; what he used to describe as 'dirty twenty-pound notes in the back pocket' was probably the main bill-payer for him.

Stand-up also became the main focus of Dermot's artistic efforts, at least for the time being. There were definite advantages to this: he could say what he wanted, without having to give a monkey's for the restrictions that were there on radio. He alone decided what was in the show. In other words, he didn't have to hold back unless he really wanted to. Also, he still loved performing and when gigs went well, he got a particular kind of rock 'n' roll adrenaline rush, which he enjoyed. When things went really well, he'd inevitably throw in new material, some that he had been working on and some quite spur-of-the-moment stuff.

Jobs for the Boys was the first tour during which Dermot really decided to play around with stand-up and devise material specifically for a show. It began in September 1993, two months before Ben was born. He wrote a whole new show for that tour and dropped the vast majority of his older material. The show was very much based on Dermot's quite visible anger at the kind of back-scratching politics, which he felt wasn't the most laudable or seemly part of a democracy. But it has always been the case in Ireland and Dermot was disgusted by it.

The show was put on at the start of the tour in the intimate surroundings of the Tivoli Theatre in Dublin's Liberties for a four-week run. But the success was so great he ended up extending the run to eight weeks. Afterwards, Dermot took the show on a tour around Ireland, which for some reason, as with most of Dermot's gigging escapades, took in the strangest and most diverse collection of venues humanly possible. It went from palatial Victorian theatres in

Cork and Waterford to possibly one of the most bizarre venues — a small pub outside Skiberreen, where he wasn't just playing in the round, but also playing from a balcony above him. It was like doing a gig in a stairwell, if that makes any sense.

Touring took a back seat then when the first series of *Father Ted* was recorded in December 1994 in London. But even with the success of *Ted*, stand-up remained an element of his career. During the second series I remember him doing a set at a comedy club in Brixton one night. But that kind of approach to stand-up was how Dermot by and large worked. He'd be busy with one thing and then all of a sudden, he'd be down the road, booting along to a gig, usually somewhere in the Irish outback.

In the early part of 1995, though, the first series of *Ted* was finished and Dermot could go back to touring and getting his own projects off the ground. He did another tour from February to April of that year, the Guinness-sponsored *Black Humour Tour*. Bloody brilliant. Dermot was over the moon at getting the sponsorship deal with the brewers. He'd been trying for a while to find some sponsorship and, obviously, a deal with the producers of his favourite drink was even better. As part of the show, he was to drink a pint of Guinness if at all possible. This doesn't mean he did a huge sell-out in the Jay-Leno-style; he didn't stand-up and say, 'Mmmm, I love Guinness, drink it, people'. There was more irony and definitely more humour involved — all more fodder for the show. For a start, Dermot dubbed it the *Guinness Black Humour Tour*. Also, the fact that Guinness had asked him to drink a pint on stage found its way into the act. Every show began with a few words on the matter:

'They asked me during the negotiations if I'd drink a pint of Guinness on stage. That held up negotiations! I'd drink a pint off Jack Charlton's arse!'

Fiona and Ben came along a lot and Bobby and I joined him from time to time — usually in far-flung places like Sligo or Cork. The prospect of getting out of Dublin to more tranquil settings and of seeing Dermot again always put us on the train.

The pattern of the show was a little bit like the previous tour, but the material was by and large new. Again it was nation-wide, but had as the main focus a week-long stint in the Olympia Theatre in Dublin, one of the city's main venues and a lot larger than the Tivoli where he had played previously. The tour involved a lot of different material, such as the notion of Michael Noonan, as Bono's Mephisto character from U2's *Zoo TV* tour, phoning up 'a war torn and godforsaken part of the world — come in Limerick!'

In general, touring was done from Dublin. If he could, Dermot would go from Dublin to wherever in the country he was performing and return that night, which meant he'd often be back at two or three in the morning. I don't think he liked being away from home for too long if he was on his own. But now and again, he did end up being away from home for more than a few nights. He also travelled abroad doing gigs. Sometimes he'd use it as an excuse for a holiday, perhaps in Cork, which, during the summer, can be like the Mediterranean in your back yard. Other times, though, he'd just go out and do a couple of gigs and be on the road with very few people. What road crew there was wasn't particularly large, in fact I don't think it ever contained more than a few people. Dermot was mainly accompanied by a single roadie, John Fisher, who was later replaced by a team of three, after John went off travelling for a year. This trio consisted of Sonya Fildes, Dermot's assistant of many years, the late Dave Jordan and Roger Reddy. Greg Ledwidge came on board later still, to replace Dave Jordan after he left. However, through the years, the two people most involved were John, who had done roadie work for Dermot for as long as I can remember and was a good friend of his, and Sonya. Together they did a lot of the long hauls, to places like Kilkenny or, on one particular occasion, Galway, where their car crashed and they had to return to Dublin feeling a bit out of place in the back seat of a bus.

The final tour Dermot did was the *Dermot Morgan Addresses the Nation* tour in 1997. This was a brand new show and played with the idea of him sweeping to power in a military coup. He came on at the beginning of the show dressed in military garb: combats, boot and sunglasses, *á la* Laurent Kabila, who had taken over in Zaire at the time, and proceeded to address the nation.

The show was a huge success and, from what I remember, it was really just Dermot and John Fisher going on tour. I don't think he really stayed anywhere overnight during that tour either: no matter how tired he was coming home, he loved to wake up in his own bed in the morning. That took up the early half of 1997, and kept him going to a large extent whilst his other projects were forming and developing. However as the year dragged on, he had a few more gigs to do.

One of these turned out to be extremely poignant for me: it was the last time I saw Dermot performing live. It was in October 1997, when he did a concert in Theatre L in UCD for the Freshers' Week celebrations, during my first year in college. I was late, running up from Booterstown to Belfield to see it. The bouncers kindly let me in through one of the side-doors to the theatre. The place was packed, so I just sat at the bottom of the steps, nearly looking up at him. It was an amazing gig. When he came out at the beginning, the audience raised the roof, banging on tables and generally giving Dermot a rousing reception, something he always enjoyed when playing there. As the gig progressed, though, I noticed Dermot moving away from the script, becoming freer and improvising more. It was an amazing sight, as the audience egged him on to do more and be truly manic, which he did without too much hesitation. I got the impression it was like a moment of release for him. It was the gig of his that I'd seen that I enjoyed the most. I didn't view it that night as 'Daddy's Job'. It was much more than that.

After the gig and a photographer from one of the college papers had taken some pictures of him, John Fisher, Dermot and I headed to the student bar for a few beers. The place was packed, so we squeezed our way up to the bar. When we got there, there was this really touching moment when the manager of the bar, Seamus Boylan — who was there when Dermot had been secretary to the bar committee as a student — and Dermot greeted each other with a huge hug, like old friends. So we proceeded to get nicely loaded. All in all it was a wonderful night and, later on, Dermot and I stuffed our faces in a small Thai restaurant in Monkstown, mulling over God and the world. That's my last memory of him gigging.

Stand and Deliver

These are samples of Dermot's stand-up routines during his last few tours. They begins with Jim, his crass 'rugger-bugger' who never really got much of an airing in public, but often did in private in the company of Pat Finn and Peter and Michael Redmond. This monologue was only performed once, at the Amnesty International comedy evening, 'So You Think You're Irish', at the Gaiety Theatre in Dublin in 1997. It comes close to the form Jim took in the pub. I was in the audience that night and it was funny watching the audience reaction to the piece, which hovered somewhere between shock, anger and sheer amusement — exactly where every stand-up should be.

Amnesty

Amnesty is a great cause because it's not nice, let's be honest, when old people start to forget things... sorry, that's Amnesia I was thinking about there.

Amnesty got onto me at the golf club and asked me to help them make an appeal tonight and when I asked what it was all about, they said it was about such issues as torture, imprisonment, capital punishment and so on. And I was delighted to help out with their appeal: it's a great cause and I am of course all in favour of torture, imprisonment and capital punishment.

My wife often says listening to me is pure torture. Tsch. Women. Fair play to them, you know. They're gas. And of course they should have equality, a certain amount of equality. The bits of equality that men don't need.

But anyhow, the wife says to me, "It's torture listening to you" so I said, "Fair play, I hear what you're saying, I hear where you're coming from on this. Do you know where this is coming from..." and I punched her. That stunned her a bit. The wife. Hah. The gas thing...is it wasn't even my wife I hit.

Wife beating is a problem for some men. Just can't do it, and it's dead easy. Think of Hitler. Strong management.

Anyway, Amnesty. Nelson Mandela. Now there's a guy I have always had a certain amount of sympathy with...him being in jail for 25 years and so on. I even watched him being released, it was live on the telly remember and getting my first glimpse of him. Well that put an end to my sympathy. Amnesty didn't bother to tell me he was black. He must have done something.

I'm not a racist. A man's colour doesn't interest me at all except in the case of Chris Evans, whose colour is offensive. He may not be black but he's a red.

Very, very red. Public hazard. Motorists get a glimpse of that red on the sidewalk and they screech to a halt, and wait half a day for him to change to green.

Not natural for someone to be that red. His testicles would look like baubles on a Christmas tree. And I for one do not want my kids to come down on Christmas morning and find Chris Evans perched in the tree with his goolies dangling between Santa and one of the fairy lights.

Oh yes, fairy lights, that bloke Oscar Wilde. A bloke was telling me the other day that he was one... you know... one of them. Now he was a guy they put in prison and they were right to. They had to. The Victorians knew what they were doing. The last thing poor old Gladstone wanted was to be leaving number 10 some day, worried about the Crimea or the Franco-Prussian war or the Battle of Hastings or what have you, I read a bit of history, and having Oscar Wilde run up and pinch his arse.

Not on, Chief. The Victorians had to put him in jail. Imagine Queen Victoria on her way to Buckingham Palace and Oscar jumps out and starts kissing one of her coachmen or something. Not on.

And then you have women's causes. I was saying to my secretary Deirdre the other day, women who go on about periods and pains that only women get, don't know what real pain is, the pain that only men get. You'd know what I mean if you ever got a kick in the balls and do you know what she said?

"And do you get a kick in the balls every month?"

I would have fired her, only she was clearly pre-menstrual and might have wrecked the office or something.

No, no, they're not afraid to answer you back nowadays. That's all because of the suffragettes. I could never agree with them. Jesus, didn't one of them throw herself under a racehorse at Ascot. Bloody irresponsible. She could have hurt that racehorse.

[THINKS] ...that's one way to get rid of period pain..

Now, I read that Queen Victoria took cannabis for her periods. Now people talk about the Queen's role in the modern world, well I can tell you what the Queen's roll in the last century was...it was a bloody big spliff is what her roll was.

I'm quite hip myself you know. My eldest lad gave me a joint once. And I'm not talking about a leg of lamb here.

He's a gas man. He was conceived around the time of that movie... Love Story... actually he was conceived during that movie Love Story and my wife Dolores decided we should call him after the star of the movie.

So we called him Ali. Fortunately, a lot of people thought we called him after Muhammad Ali who is of course black and who is now sadly so uncoordinated and brain-damaged that people are starting to say he should be picked for the Irish rugby team.

Anyway Ali, my eldest lad...Gave me a joint and it did nothing for me. But apparently you're not supposed to eat it. So he gave me another one and I smoked it and that did nothing for me either...I just gave up on drugs there and then and went off and settled for three bowls of Coco Pops and some cold rashers I found in the fridge with a mustard sandwich and chocolate digestives with pate on them instead.

Anyway, Amnesty, torture, jail, capital punishment... I'm here to say... Yes... I'm for all of them.

The Guinness Black Humour Tour

The following are extracts from Dermot Morgan Live, *a recording of a performance in the Olympia Theatre, Dublin during the Guinness Black Humour Tour, 1995*

It's great to be here. The nice thing about working in Dublin and working in my own hometown is that I don't have to go through some of the more interesting cultural centres in the provinces to get here. Now normally when I'm going to a gig I have to use one of two axis. And the first town if you're doing Galway that kind of direction is Kinnegad! See you're laughing already. But then you don't have to go through it! Kinnegad is one of those really interesting places — I have to go through Kinnegad sometimes — I try to do it at speed! I think if God was going to give Ireland an enema the tube would be fed into Kinnegad.

Now the other option, usually is to have to go through Mountrath. Now let me tell you about Mountrath. I'm very popular with the Laois constabulary — having boosted the courts funds down there as is my wont. I was caught doing 90 MPH going through Mountrath, now have you seen Mountrath? 90 isn't half-shagging fast enough I'm telling you!

✵

One person I know will never be stuck for a job will be Mike Murphy. Our premier Arts Presenter and Lotto Bingo Caller! Have you seen the cardboard cut-out of him in the Lotto shops? *(Imitating Mike Murphy)* Its gas isn't it... ha... ha...' It's far more realistic than the real thing. At least the cardboard cut-out has two dimensions!

☆

Show business and the old politics, you have to be very careful, cause there's a lot of similarities between show business and politics. It's like being a cabinet minister, it's about the same thing as being in U2! You get your own driver and the chance to do your own show every day! That's what the Dáil is, a show — it's a fecking disgrace as it happens! But I've picked up a few trips... a Freudian slip!... I've picked up a few tricks from Bono and we're going to try them out here tonight. We have the technology, we have the satellites, we're going to try to establish here tonight... on the stage of the Olympia, Dublin's premier theatre, a live phone-link with a certain war-torn, violence-ravaged city which is never far from our thoughts... Come in Limerick! No answer they must be at an away game in Glenamaddy. Four roads to Glenamaddy ane they're all jammed with ambulances.

☆

Our future is in Europe, there's no question in this. Some things have changed in Europe, for example the Berlin Wall is down. I know because I made an offer for it. I was going to build it around Limerick... you know like. Get a kind of Auschwitz theme park going. "We are a goot time having, ya?"

The Germans are in a very, very commanding position in Europe. They are re-united. And who's to say they won't go for third time lucky... so there is only one way... one way to guarantee peace in our time and that is to give Ireland to the Germans and we take Germany. Now you just follow the logic in this for a while... if you were in Poland in September 1939 and you were waiting for the Irish to invade, you would be waiting, wouldn't you. If you saw the Irish pouring across your border, you'd know there was a football match in Warsaw, Jack Charlton was bringing his guys in, that's the only reason. We are not an aggressive people — despite what I said about Limerick. I mean we couldn't have won the Battle of Britain.

"Bandits, six o'clock, scramble the Spitfires."

"Ah, now. I couldn't, that's not my job, that's his job. No I couldn't."

"Now listen here, the Hun is about to threaten our Homeland. Get in that Spitfire and shoot the bastard down."

"Oh no, I couldn't do that. If I touch that machine gun, everybody's out. That's a machine gunner's job. I'm in SIPTU."

Peace in our time guaranteed by the Irish.

☆

There's been a lot of talk here tonight about jobs for the boys. I used to have a good song about Nelson Mandela — then b'jeazus they released him. You can laugh, I lost a song. Great song about the Birmingham Six, they're out. Guilford Four they're gone. Release Nicky Kelly, he's out. If this goes on there'll be no songs left.

There's one man being hounded by the Fascist Free State police force. And they eventually put him away because of his love of the freedom of the roads, freedom from licence, taxation and insurance. When they eventually put him behind bars at least I'll have a song out of it.

> In Mountjoy Jail one Monday morning,
> A silence fell and hushed the din.
> And the prisoners turned and looked on
> as they brought Eamonn Dunphy in.
>
> The Cons nearly caused a riot,
> who'll have to share a cell with him?
> Get him out before tonight,
> then the Cons began to sing:

179

Release the little bollix in D Wing,
get him out of here I hear them sing.
The windows they are banging,
get him out or bring back hanging.
Release the little bollix in D Wing.

Now history has seen many famous heroes,
locked away behind a ten-foot wall.
But you should have heard the roar,
for the man who once played midfield for Millwall.

They locked up the great Nelson Mandela,
they put away poor Oscar for being wild.
But compared to being locked up with Dunphy,
I'd say that Reading Gaol was fairly mild.

Rudolph Hess was likewise fairly lucky,
Dunphy less they jailed him in Berlin.
Luckiest of all was Nicky Kelly,
He got out before they put old Eammo in.

Release the little bollix in D Wing,
get him out of here I hear them sing.
The windows they are banging,
get him out or bring back hanging.
Release the little bollix in D Wing.

So they put old Eamonn in with a murderer,
a man who was going down for life.
Who turned to him and said " Well hello blondie."
"How do you feel about being my new wife?"

So Eamonn started talking about Liam Brady,
and attacking Miller, Donagh and Stapleton.
John Hume, Jackie Charlton, Mrs. Robinson,
you know the list it just goes on and on.

Now the psycho in the cell who fancied Eamo,
had to suffer this tirade the whole damn night.
When dawn broke over Phibsboro next morning,
poor sod was swinging gently from the light.

Release the little bollix in D wing,
get him out of here I hear them sing.
The windows they are banging,
get him out or bring back hanging.
Release the little bollix in D Wing.

Now the next night in his prison cell in Mountjoy,
Eamonn was lying wide awake.
When the warder knocked and said "Congratulations,
the prisoners and the staff baked you this cake."

But soon his tooth hit something and his face creased,
then it broke into a ready smile.
" How thoughtful of the governor and the prisoners,
they've even sent me in a metal file."

Beside the file a note was neatly folded,
he nearly swallowed it, it made him cough
to read the words "the gates have been left open,
kindly take the hint and please fuck off."

(Last time, altogether, everybody in the Olympia)

Release the little bollix in D Wing,
get him out of here I hear them sing.
The windows they are banging,
get him out or bring back hanging.
Release the little bollix in D Wing.

Goodnight, God bless you and thank you very much.

IT'S NOT YOUR FAULT...

by Bobby Morgan

Dermot taught me many different things in this life, and perhaps the most fun thing he ever taught me was how to have a good night out. The first thing I saw after birth was the bottom of a champagne bottle and this set the tone for many nights of fun that would follow. Anyone who thinks that a father teaching his son to drink is a bad thing, think again. Not only was he an ideal father in the time he spent with us as kids but, as we grew, he was prepared to let us grow. He always believed that the good things in life were best in small, controlled doses. This was something he taught to us at an early age.

I can remember the pride Dermot took in giving us a glass of wine with our lunch on weekends, or at dinner. It made him proud that we were mature enough to drink wine with him, while other parents were still fretting about what their children would do after one glass of cola. Of course it made us extremely proud that he trusted us not to make a spectacle of ourselves. After all, how many parents would give their children a half-glass of wine before they were thirteen years old? That's what set him apart as a parent.

There were few things he demanded in his life, but he saw it as his duty to ensure that he bought us our first pints of the black stuff, so guaranteeing that an Irish rite of passage was upheld. I can still remember the pomp and circumstance with which a pint of dirty looking, black liquid with a crisp white head was placed in front of me in a bar in Ennis, County Clare. Originally it was only supposed to have been Don's first pint, but after sufficient whinging about the inequality of it all, I too was given a pint of the good stuff. And with that nights out on the town were made possible, in fact that night in Ennis was the first one where the drink was taken in a pub as opposed to a restaurant, over dinner.

That occasion allowed for a far more open style of night out. Football matches were now the source of much merriment and we downed pints of stout along with everyone else. The summer of 1994 brought with it a World Cup campaign and the by now infamous 'hi-ho' incident in the Senor Sassis restaurant in Dublin's Leeson Street, where a large number of us ended up dancing around the floor on our knees. That was an innocuous enough occurrence when compared with the events later in the night when, whilst worshipping at the porcelain altar, I was quoted as saying "It's not your fault, Popsey". It also saw Dermot regret for the first time his decision to treat us like responsible young adults. However, even in the cold light of day he decided that we were still a good risk and he continued to treat us like equals.

It was not only football that brought alcohol with it; his two *Guinness Black Humour* tours showed once again the trust and faith he had in us. I remember how one night after a particularly good run in the Tivoli Theatre he had booked a function room in the Burlington Hotel. He laid on an excellent spread of food, drink and invited a lot of people to celebrate yet another success. It was here that he was given the chance to be the sensible parent as well as the adventurous one. I can remember clearly how a man, the origin of his invitation undisclosed, made some comment about the suit I was wearing. At the time I had an inclination towards violence as a solution to my problems and I had been prepared to hit this character. However my father, ever alert, intervened to stop me from making a show of the party. It was that which made him such a perfect father: he could be laughing, drinking, having fun one minute, and defending his sons from themselves the next.

However, Don and I would never tolerate such sentimentality on a long-term basis and the tours that followed were the source of more rites of passage. On one memorable occasion after the end of a stretch in the Olympia Theatre, we had all gone for dinner at La Stampa, where once again Dermot sat there practically glowing with pride at the behaviour of his two sons. In fact so impressed was he with our performance that he decided to bring us with him to his favourite night-time haunt, Lillie's Bordello. This was a scene straight out of an opera: Don and I were led in by Dermot as though we were being led into the underworld. However the hours spent there passed off without incident, in spite of my only being fifteen. That was trust.

That was perhaps the biggest thing for Dermot: trust. Rarely did Don or I betray it. Only once in his presence did Don and I not repay the confidence he had invested in us. It was the Christmas following the filming of the first series of *Father Ted* in 1994. Don and I had been invited to the wrap party in Waterloo Fire Station. Dermot let us off the leash and Don and I consumed every sort of beer in the place. This was not a wise move and resulted in Dermot sending us home in a taxi. Not one of our finest hours and needless to say a certain amount of trust was lost forever.

However, alcohol was not all that Dermot had in common with us, but it was the universal healer. It also gave him immense pleasure to aid us in any of our pursuits, such as the first time he saw me wearing the goal-keeping helmet he had bought me for hockey, and even more so when I joined Pembroke Wanderers hockey club, only a stone's throw from his home. He didn't only support us in our sporting pursuits, but our musical ones too. He bought Don his first drum-kit and sticks and followed that a year later by buying me my first bass guitar. These were things he lived for. He loved to see Don, Ben or I do something that he had helped us with and it hurt him when he couldn't be part of them. I remember how proud I was of him when he came to collect me from hockey one Saturday in November 1997. He told me that he had just been in the Berkeley Court Hotel and that on his way out Liam Gallagher of Oasis had stopped him and invited him to go to a party with them. Dermot declined, saying that he had to collect me. That was the best feeling in the world.

Things like that reminded you how real he was. He never lost the head about his status, even if I got a kick out of it. On the second-last occasion that I saw him alive, we met in Dublin city centre and I asked him if he had time for dinner that evening. Luckily he did and he brought me to Planet Hollywood. I arrived half-an-hour before him and was told that I would have to wait that long to be seated. I didn't mind, but when Dermot finally arrived, the hostess took me to one side and told me that she could have seated me immediately if I had told her who would be joining me. I loved that kind of feeling, but Dermot didn't care. He never used his status as an excuse to demand special treatment and never would have either. He was happy enough to meet his idols, people like Ruud Gullit. The photo which was taken of the two at the Q Magazine awards in London was his little thrill. He made some new friends who had a public profile, but he never forgot his old friends or his family. He had time for everyone, even if we didn't always have time for him.

The last time I saw him was one such occasion. I had just returned from Hamburg and he planned to fly to England the next morning. However, he still sacrificed his own need to sleep to meet Don, Susanne and myself in O'Reilly's Bar in Sandymount. It was typical of him: once again he put his family first. Little did he know how important it would prove on that occasion. Even when he was in London, he never let more than two days pass without speaking to us. Ironically the night of his death was two days after I had spoken with him last. Having gone out that night I had resolved to phone him the next morning. Something I never managed.

Dermot was a model father, who had put his family ahead of work for as long as I can remember. He taught Don and I to be strong in important company and he gave us Ben. What he taught Ben I don't know, but it will have been as invaluable as that which he taught us. Wherever he is now, he is still looking after Don, Ben and me.

DERMOT THE FATHER

by Fiona Clarke

To be loved by Dermot was incredible and so, losing him is totally devastating. There are no words to describe it and there is nothing anyone can do to take away the pain. I just loved him so much and now he is gone.

Chris de Burgh wrote in Dermot's condolence book: 'Thank you for the gift of love that you have left behind… the best legacy any of us can aspire to.' Dermot as a father and as a partner had such an enormous capacity for love. I often felt humbled by his ability to see through the crap of every day life and just love. He loved his three sons totally and completely. He was so proud of the wonderful men Don and Bobby had become and he desperately hoped that he would 'see Ben up'. Dermot didn't have time to do that, but the four years that Ben did have with him and the gift of love he has left behind will be with Ben forever.

When Ben was born, I was checking fingers and toes and wondering what were those white spots on his nose, and would the red mark on his face disappear; Dermot just held him and kissed him and repeated over and over again: 'He's so beautiful, he's just so beautiful.'

Dermot was the father who carried Ben down to school on his shoulders in the mornings; who when Ben had gone into school, hid behind the hedge to check that he was OK; who phoned on his mobile phone to make sure he was OK;

and who cried his way through the Christmas plays. He was such a huge presence in Ben's life. They spent hours wrestling, making up stories, playing football, going for walks and sometimes just sitting together in the car looking at the sea.

Ben was always sure of Dermot's love.

Dermot was a brilliant man and he fought hard for so much in his life. Nothing came to him the easy way — he never gave in and he never gave up and he never became bitter — angry, but not bitter. He was strongly driven by a need to protect, to care and to provide for those he loved. If Dermot was on your side — nothing or nobody could ever get you!

To continue to be here without Dermot often seems too hard, but I know that Ben and myself are the luckiest people on this earth to have had such a love in our lives.

THE BESTEST DADDY

by Ben Morgan

Dermot Morgan died, and he was my Dad and I loved him so much. He was the funniest man in the world and everybody loved him. He was the bestest Daddy in the whole world. I liked all the jokes he told and I loved it when he played Father Ted on the television coz it's really funny. I'm so sad that he died and I wish he didn't have a heart attack and die and I miss him. I didn't want him to die because he was my Dad and I loved him more than anyone.

This is all the stuff about my Dad.

Love from Ben.

'TID' and 'DOODLE'

It was in the Unicorn Restaurant in Dublin that I first heard of *Father Ted*. That must have been around 1992 or 1993, just when Dermot's radio show on Dublin station, 98FM, was running in the mornings and his stand-up show, *Jobs For the Boys*, was about to take off. Dermot had asked me if I wanted to come into town and have some lunch. On the way in, he told me that some of the lunch would be taken up with business. 'I have to meet this guy, Arthur Matthews,' he said, or words to that effect. Arthur and his writing partner, Graham Linehan, are two Irish writers who had started out working for *Hot Press* in Dublin. By the time *Ted* had come into being, they had already written material for the cream of British comedy; the likes of Smith and Jones and Steve Coogan, aka Alan Partridge.

This particular afternoon was vaguely grey, or at least, it looked like that in the dark surroundings of the old Unicorn Restaurant. We met Arthur, a very articulate guy who told Dermot about this idea he and Graham had for a series about three priests stuck on an island off the West coast of Ireland. That's as much as I remember of that afternoon. The next time I heard about it was when Dermot told me it had been given the go-ahead by Channel 4.

When he got the scripts, Dermot was struck by the quality of them. They were brilliant, as far as he was concerned; he just laughed and laughed at their humour. That said, something was nagging at the back of his mind.

Would it work? Would it be a success, or would it be a flop? Was it maybe a little left of field for some people? He was sure of it being funny and he took a lot of pride in praising the often wonderfully demented humour of Arthur and Graham. Nevertheless, he was unsure about how it would work out. It was obviously a good series, but would it be a hit? His insecurity was something some friends noticed as well, like Barry Devlin:

> When Dermot was at his most diffident about projects, that's when they were always best. So he wasn't sure about [Thank You Very Much] Mr. Eastwood and I just went 'It's brilliant.' I remembered this when he brought me in to see the first episode of Father Ted, and I've never seen him as diffident in all my life. Normally he'd be going 'God, it's brilliant, Baz!' but he was going, 'I dunno. I think the writing's brilliant. I think Arthur and Graham, the two lads, are brilliant, but I dunno. Will people get this?' I'm going, 'Please don't put me through this, Dermot. If you're this diffident, it must be terrible.' But four minutes in I'm going 'Hold on a sec... this is Steptoe and Son, this is Fawlty Towers' — a complete break of the mould.

It soon became clear, when the first series was broadcast, that Father Ted would take off, allaying the fears Dermot, or indeed anyone, may have had about it being understood. As far as I remember, it was soon a cult series in Britain, especially with students and in the Irish community. It was the break Dermot had been craving for years, and its success was due in no small part to the talents of those who worked with him on the show, as well as Dermot's unique skill in playing Ted. As Declan Lowney remembers: 'It wasn't like an actor (playing the part), there was something else going on.'

Filming *Father Ted* meant that there would be a lot of travel: to London for the studio scenes and out into the West of Ireland, in the bleakness of the Burren in County Clare, for all of the exterior shots. Dermot hated the cold and wet days around Lahinch and Enistymon in Clare, where people called Ted and Ardal O'Hanlon's character, Dougal, 'Tid and Doodle'. On one occasion, they were so sick of eating chicken and chips that Dermot phoned up a pizza place in Ennis and ordered pizza to be driven out for everyone on the set. On the other hand, he loved London although I don't think he particularly wanted all the upheaval involved in the travelling back and forth. Most complaints of having to travel here, there and everywhere subsided, however, as he found himself in a particular variation of what was his element.

Dermot, his partner Fiona, and Ben lived in London during the periods when he was filming there. He lived in St Margaret's, near Richmond, just down the road from his sister, Denise, which meant he could see her a lot more and Ben had friends to play with, in the shape of our cousins, Denise and Declan's kids: Simon, Ruth, Eoin and Stephen.

Although Dermot settled down after a while and began to enjoy things in London, he would often be gagging to get back to Dublin. There were a few reasons for this but one of the main ones was that he missed, without equivocation or qualification, playing footie with his mates. He missed running around a gym with the other members of The Committee, people like Donagh Morgan, Pat Finn, Peter Redmond, Noel Boyce and that whole crowd. I remember that being one of the things he would go on about when he first went over to London. He wondered if he could find a football game to play in there. He didn't, but when he came back to Dublin, he was as happy as Larry, getting back into the game. I guess he also missed watching League of Ireland football down in UCD with his mates, and Bobby and I missed him. He got to see some Premiership football in London and soon became a Chelsea fan, something that Ben has also become (although when he was smaller he was quite partial to the occasional Leeds United chant). Ben was growing to love football, something Dermot readily encouraged, taking him to see Fulham play when they were living around the corner from Fulham's home ground for a time, an experience which, Dermot told me at the time, they both enjoyed.

Another thing he complained a lot about was the beer in England. He found it fascinating and drank bitter in the Turk's Head in St Margaret's and places like that with Denise's husband, Declan. But, to be honest, he missed his pints of Guinness with his friends in Doheny & Nesbitt's bar in Dublin, or in the pub after footie.

As much as he missed Ireland, though, he made the most of his time in England. He explored what was a relatively unknown place to him, and he used to find all these amazing little eateries to which he would subsequently bring Bobby and I when we went over to visit him. That was all a lot of fun.

The way *Father Ted* was rehearsed was fascinating. For a start, it seemed to be incredibly relaxed as I witnessed in the couple of episodes I saw in preparation for shooting. Here's an example. In the second series, there was the infamous plague of rabbits episode, possibly one of the best. I had my Easter holidays that week, so I went over to see Dermot, whom I hadn't seen since he had gone over to London about a month previously. I went with him in the morning to Soho where the rehearsal rooms were, right on the top floor. The director, Declan Lowney, the other production people and the other cast members, Pauline, Ardal and

Frank, were sitting around, pretty relaxed. I was expecting mild panic at the prospect of having to get a show rehearsed in preparation for recording in front of an audience the following Friday. But it was quite the opposite. I went off for most of the morning, doing touristy stuff, and came back at lunchtime. Again, they seemed to be extremely relaxed. The following day was even better. They had a rabbit brought in to rehearse with. It was funny watching as everyone took turns cuddling the little furry animal.

Professionally, that time in his life was one of Dermot's happiest, I think. He was getting somewhere in television and he was getting recognised by the business in London. One of the things that *Ted* brought him on his arrival on the scene in England was recognition of how good he was. That was recognised formally when he was voted Best Comic Actor at the annual British Comedy Awards in 1997. He got a huge, huge kick out of that. Come to think of it, being in London gave him several kicks, such as meeting people he would otherwise never have encountered, like the Republic of Ireland football manager Mick McCarthy, who became a good friend. Indeed, shortly before Dermot died he said he'd introduce me to him when I was next over there, a prospect to which I looked forward.

In between the series of *Ted*, Dermot concentrated on his own stuff, which he was looking to further — suddenly a more tangible prospect with the success of *Ted*. He developed his idea for the novel about international terrorists kidnapping Franz Beckenbauer, *The Kaiser Conspiracy*. He was writing more and more and producing some great scripts, including one or two great screenplays that were in progress. There was also something of a change from the past in what he was writing. Previously, he had written material to perform himself, but he was now moving away from that and writing more things that he did not see himself playing.

Two of the screenplays were based on episodes in Irish history. One was called *The Curragh Colditz*, a drama series for BBC about the Allied and German servicemen who were imprisoned together in the Curragh in County Kildare because of Irish neutrality during World War Two. It was the one and only time Barry Devlin and Dermot were formally going to collaborate on scripts. Unlike their earlier efforts at collaboration, Barry says:

> I think it would've probably worked out all right, because both of us had learned a great deal. He particularly had become very disciplined about his work. The key part to me in *Curragh Colditz* was that of the camp Commandant which was patently him and yet he didn't want to play it, because he wanted to write and he didn't want that to be adulterated (by any other influence).

The other screenplay was about an incident in the fifties, when the Archbishop of Dublin at the time, John Charles McQuaid, attempted to ban a match between Ireland and Yugoslavia. Dermot changed the visiting team to Hungary and the screenplay was named *The Miracle of the Magyars*. So as *Ted* was running and there was no filming to be done, that was what was occupying Dermot's time: what his next step was going to be. That and catching up with things in Dublin, going to Doheny's and different places, or just going out to the Pigeon House at Dublin Bay and looking out to sea, something he did a lot. Sometimes Bobby, Ben or I went with him but mostly he went there on his own.

By that time *Ted* was taking off in Ireland as well, especially when RTÉ bought it. Dermot was becoming instantly recognisable to many people and he loved it as much as he hated it, ever-protective of his privacy as he was. It must have been an uncomfortable feeling when someone would come up to him in a bookshop and scream 'Feck, arse, drink' at him. Sometimes, though, it was a hoot. There are two stories which illustrate this particularly well. The first is an incident which happened on German Reunification Day, October 3rd, in St Kilian's, the German school in Dublin that Bobby and I attended. Helmut Kohl, Germany's Chancellor at the time, was in Dublin and his wife Hannelore came to the school to hand out state-sponsored German language certificates, *Sprachdiploms*, to the pupils who had passed the exam. Bobby was going to be awarded with his that day and the band I was in at the time, *Pale Lounger*, had been asked to play afterwards. Dermot was due to turn up to see these two events. Frau Kohl came in and everything was extremely formal and nice. Dermot wasn't there yet, late as usual. Then, sitting in the audience, I could see Dermot looking down into the gym, where the event was happening, from the canteen overlooking it. As the ceremony went on, Dermot came down to see Bobby receive his *Sprachdiplom*, after which my band was to go on. He was standing at the back, inconspicuously, with some of the teachers when all of a sudden some kids saw Dermot and mobbed him for his autograph, totally spontaneously, and, I might add, upstaging Frau Kohl! It was the funniest sight watching two of the teachers, Fiona Holly and Regina O'Reilly, trying to bring some order to things. Dear, oh dear...

The other incident happened after an international football match that Dermot attended with John Fisher around the time he was becoming friends with Mick McCarthy. After the match there was a 'do' where Dermot was mobbed by people wanting his autograph in front of an RTÉ executive with whom he had had some run-ins over the years. As he was signing the autographs, he could see the RTÉ man's face peering over at the crowd around him. Dermot balanced the autograph books he was signing on two fingers, aimed straight at him. Sweet victory...

There was a lot of time between the second and third series of *Ted*. Dermot came back to Ireland and did his *Addresses the Nation* tour. Along with that, he was progressing with the different scripts he'd been working on, like a sit-com set in the Dutch embassy in London called *Going Dutch*, which he was co-writing with Nick Revell. *The Curragh Colditz* was also coming along well. As time went by and winter arrived, the preparations for the third series of *Ted* had begun and not long after Christmas 1997, he was off down to Clare again to do the exterior shots. After a few weeks, they were back for a short time before they had to go to London to record the studio footage.

The night before he left for London, we all met up for a few pints in O'Reilly's in Sandymount — Dermot, Bobby, Mum and me. We had a nice time, although he was quite tired, and we chatted about this and that — it was great. After exchanges of hugs and promises of getting together really soon, we went in our separate directions.

That was the last time we saw him alive. We spoke regularly over the phone afterwards and I was going to go over to see him when my Easter break from college began, the week after the series was wrapped up. The day I should have gone over to London was the day of his funeral.

There's a story a friend of mine told me around the time of the funeral. He was working in RTÉ the Sunday the news that Dermot had died broke. As a mark of respect, they wanted to forgo showing the episode of *Father Ted* intended for that day. Instead they put on a repeat of... *One Foot In the Grave* of all things! Apparently there was a moment of silent despair when they had seen what they had done.

Ted was the final thing that Dermot completed in his career. When the last shot was taken and everything was done, he looked to the future, probably wondering what his next steps would be. Instead of that future, he died the following night. That began the strangest, but most oddly comforting, weeks I've ever experienced; from the moment that our uncle Paul arrived to tell Bobby and me what had happened; to Donagh, Stef, Eoin, and Pat Finn arriving that night; to our friends living in our house for the next week.

They moved in on Sunday. I don't know who was the first, though I remember a friend of mine, Michael Donald, standing on the doorstep looking grave, something that would happen to everyone as the week went on.

Bobby and I didn't go to London. The Committee did, to bring him back.

Meanwhile, our friends demonstrated what warm, weird and wonderful people they are. They brought joy into the house with their quick-fire joking, bringing life into what would otherwise have been a place filled with death.

They demonstrated their generosity as well, be it Barry Meggs taking over the cooking and being dubbed 'the bitch in the kitchen', or Leo Speßhardt, a friend of mine for years, making it over for the funeral from Liverpool at the very last minute.

Those were the high points for us in Dublin. There were many, many lows. One of the many was walking up to the altar during the funeral with the offertory gifts: Ben between Bobby and me. This small guy, our brother, who would grow up without Dermot around.

It's kind of funny but the days leading up to and including the funeral were a clear demonstration as to what Dermot had achieved. In forty-five years he touched many,

many different people with his humour, his warmth and his love and outright passion for life and the things he believed in. He had come from a childhood in 1950s Dublin, survived the Christian Brothers and gone through college and onwards, his talents blooming, a person who could do so much, enjoy so much as well as suffer so much. And he had so much more he wanted to do.

One of his heroes, John Cleese said about Graham Chapman, 'He died before he'd had enough fun.' That's probably a good summing up, too, for Dermot Morgan — our father.

AFTERWORD

By Donagh Morgan

'Dermot Morgan is dead'. These were the words of the announcer on one of our national radio stations on Sunday, 1 March, 1998, which told the country of Dermot's death. The words themselves are cold but reflect the shock of the enormity of what we were being told. What meaning can death have in terms of the life-force that was Dermot? Does it have any meaning? Does it have any reality? I don't have any answers to these questions and like you I am simply trying to come to terms with his loss. I would share with you a reflection of what Dermot's life meant to me.

Dermot was a man of many passions. If he were reading this, he might suggest I was going to talk dirty about him! He was driven by his passions. He worked hard, he played hard and he loved hard.

From my earliest recollection he always wanted to perform, but more than that he wanted to write. Unlike most of us who are waiting to find out what we want to be when we grow up, he had a clear vision of where he wanted to go. This began to manifest itself in UCD with gigs like *Big Gom and the Imbeciles*. It developed through sending in scripts to Mike Murphy's early morning radio programme to the creation of Father Trendy and other characters on *The Live Mike* TV programme.

His writing talent came to maturity with *Scrap Saturday*. I recall him playing the tape of the first show for me as we drove around town in the monster Citroën that he had at that time. He was really excited about the show and knew that he had hit on something special. The excitement was infectious and was symptomatic of the energy that he put into his work. I was privileged to watch himself and Gerry Stembridge go through the preparations for writing a *Scrap* script one evening over gallons of coffee in the Elephant & Castle restaurant. To say that creative sparks were flying would be an understatement.

The deadly accuracy of the perception that he brought to *Scrap* caused me no end of unease as I was working in the Department of the Taoiseach at the time Charles Haughey was being lampooned! Dermot gave me a preview in the shower after indoor football every Friday night of what would be in the programme next morning. Suggestions of a 'Deep Throat' in the Taoiseach's Office were difficult to fend off!

Father Ted ensured that his talent would be recognised outside these shores. Dermot knew that he had cracked it when he began to be recognised by London's taximen who were greeting him in best cockney with 'Hello Favver Ted'. The same driven energy went into his work on *Ted* and he was really chuffed when this was recognised with the British Comedy Award in 1997 for top TV comedy actor.

If Dermot was passionate about his work he was equally passionate about his football, whether it was following the fortunes of the Irish team or UCD or playing indoor five-a-side. He was delighted when Ireland got to the big time for the first time by reaching the finals of the European Championships in Germany in 1988. He was unable to attend any of the games but that did not deter him from visiting all the empty stadia where the Irish team was to play later that summer. He supplemented these trips to the stadia with visits to the death camps such as Dachau and Bergen-Belsen — must have been a great holiday for his family!

Dermot put the same energy into playing five-a-side as into everything else he did. The five-a-side worked on a number of different levels. There were those of us who were there to play the beautiful game, although the beautiful game lost something in the translation from conception to execution. It was also a release valve for a highly stressed bunch of maniacs who could get rid of their aggression twice a week after work instead of going home to kick the cat/wife/kids. In an interview a number of years ago in the *Evening Press*, Dermot spoke of his enjoyment of indoor football and 'how his friends helped him to keep his feet on the ground'. Some bunch of friends. We slagged him mercilessly about this and kept throwing the quote back at him particularly in recent times when the fame that *Father Ted* brought would lead to queues forming for his autograph when he was trying to watch UCD play at Belfield. I know that it may seem a contradiction in terms to speak of queues at a UCD game when the conventional wisdom is that they are only supported by two men and a dog, but it is true.

If Dermot enjoyed playing five-a-side, he enjoyed even more the excuse it gave for going for a pint afterwards — not that any excuse was ever needed when it came to going for pints. Different things will spark off different memories but I was struck forcibly when I saw the bench and the barrels outside Doheny & Nesbitt's public house this summer. When they appeared Dermot would declare summer officially open, and it was time to play.

Many will recall the dreaded phone call from Dermot enquiring if you were free for a 'tea-timer'. This would inevitably lead to badness and more than likely a low output at work the next day. No — don't worry, I am not going to bore you with drinking stories, suffice to say that Dublin is a vibrant city and was Dermot's city and his energy contributed to that vibrancy.

Above everything Dermot's greatest passion was his family. He loved his sons, Don and Bobby, and was fortunate to see them grow up to be his pals. When he and Fiona had Ben his life was complete. In the quiet moments, which were rare and precious, he would speak of his love for his family and often he was overwhelmed by it.

And so what's left to be said? At the time of his funeral and since, people have shared with me their memories of Dermot. You all have your particular memories, each individual, each special. It made me realise how public a figure he had become and how everybody owned a little part of him.

Among the many memories, I will recall speaking to him a week before he died. He was looking forward to finishing the *Ted* series. He felt it was the best yet and would be a jumping off point for greater things. He was alive with ideas for more projects and some of them were advanced enough that hopefully they can be yet brought to fruition. He wanted to crack the big time. What he didn't know was that he had already done so. We are left with the sadness of unfulfilled ambition but we have the consolation of the memories.

Dermot was given a police motorcycle escort on his final journey to Glasnevin — his final gig! It was lunch-time on a Friday crossing the city. He would have taken great pleasure from bringing the traffic to a standstill and from the crowds on the sidewalks who applauded as he passed. Nice finish!